Hamlyn all-colour p

Fossils and Fossil Collecting

Roger Hamilton

Crockett
64 Whalesmead
road

Illustrated by
Ralph S. Coventry Associates
J. Baker, E. Murphy, P. Turner

Hamlyn
London · New York · Sydney · Toronto

FOREWORD

This guide is an introduction to the study of fossils, their collecting and their importance. Life probably originated on Earth over 3 200 million years ago and the many diverse groups of animals and plants that we see around us have resulted from the gradual evolution of living things over this unimaginably long period of time. Fossils provide direct evidence of the changes that have occurred to the animals and plants during the history of the Earth and they give important clues to the ancestry and relationships of living things.

The collecting of fossils can be an interesting and rewarding pastime which will greatly enhance the collector's knowledge and understanding of the Earth and the organisms that live upon it.

W.R.H.

The publishers gratefully acknowledge the assistance given to the artists by the Merseyside County Museums.

Published by The Hamlyn Publishing Group Limited
London · New York · Sydney · Toronto
Astronaut House, Feltham, Middlesex, England

Copyright © The Hamlyn Publishing Group Limited 1975
ISBN 0 600 33560 7

Phototypeset by Filmtype Services Limited, Scarborough, England
Colour separation by Metric Reproductions Limited,
Chelmsford, Essex, England
Printed in Spain by Mateu Cromo, Madrid

CONTENTS

INTRODUCTION

What is a fossil ?

Fossils are the remains of animals and plants that are preserved in the rocks. They may consist of the complete organism, just its hard parts or even just its impression. Alternatively, they may be simply traces of past life such as footprints, burrows or borings.

Life has existed on the Earth for about 3 200 million years and during this vast span of time an enormous variety of animals and plants has existed. Throughout geological time rocks have been broken down by the action of the sun, wind, water or ice and the materials released by this breakdown have been deposited to form new (sedimentary) rocks. Occasionally, organisms were trapped during the deposition of these sediments and their remains were preserved as fossils.

The Earth is estimated to be about 4 600 million years old while the oldest rocks yet discovered are approximately 3 800 million years old and occur in Greenland. The earliest evidence of life is contained in rocks from Swaziland, southern Africa that are about 3 200 million years old and are thought to contain the remains of minute plants. The oldest rocks from Britain occur in north-west Scotland and are almost 3 000 million years old while the oldest British fossils are contained in pebbles from north-west Scotland that are probably at least 1 500 million years old. Fossils only become common, however, in rocks of Cambrian or later age and for the last 600 million years the history of life is documented by a fairly complete fossil record.

Geological time

Geological time is split into several major divisions or **eras** of which the last three – Palaeozoic, Mesozoic and Caenozoic – contain the vast majority of known fossils. The eras are divided into **periods** which are themselves sub-divided into **stages**. The terms Lower, Middle and Upper are used to refer to rocks within a period while the terms early, middle and late may refer to time within a period or era; however, the terms are not interchangeable. For example, it is correct to say that the earliest mammals occur in the Upper Triassic – i.e., in Upper Triassic rocks – or that the mammals originated in late Triassic times, but it is not correct to say that the mammals originated in Upper Triassic times.

Geological time-scale

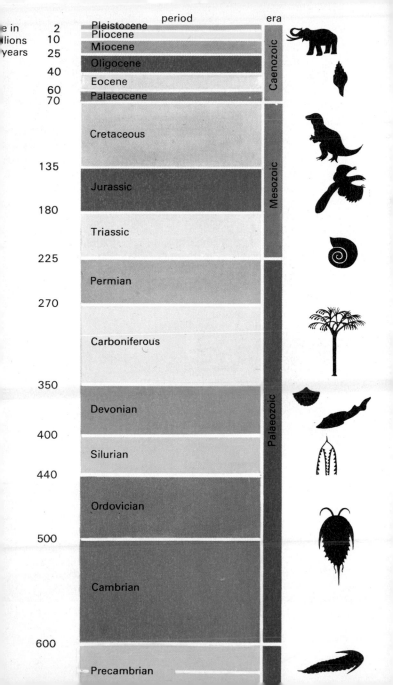

e in llions years	period	era
2	Pleistocene	Caenozoic
10	Pliocene	
25	Miocene	
40	Oligocene	
60	Eocene	
70	Palaeocene	
	Cretaceous	Mesozoic
135	Jurassic	
180	Triassic	
225	Permian	Palaeozoic
270	Carboniferous	
350	Devonian	
400	Silurian	
440	Ordovician	
500	Cambrian	
600	Precambrian	

How fossils form

Fossils represent only a tiny fraction of the total number of animals and plants that have existed as there are several conditions all of which must be fulfilled before fossilization is possible. The chances that an organism will be fossilized are greatly increased if it has hard parts, such as a shell, bones or a test, as these are more resistant to the processes of breakdown such as scavengers, bacterial action, weathering or water action. Even hard parts will be broken down relatively rapidly if they are not protected and it is therefo e necessary for the remains to be buried quickly after the death of the organism. Then the deposits must be chemically suitable for fossilization and when these deposits are formed into rocks it is necessary for the rocks to survive to allow the survival of the fossils that they contain. If all these conditions occur then there is a chance that organisms will be fossilized and it is amazing that so many fossils occur to provide us with a detailed record of the history of animals and plants.

living animal

hard parts of dead animal

rapid burial

impregnation by minerals from sediments

chalk

limestone

sandstone

shale

Sedimentary rocks

Throughout geological time rocks have been broken down and the particles resulting from this breakdown have been redeposited to form sedimentary rocks. All fossils are found in sedimentary rocks and, as these are usually deposited in water, the remains of aquatic animals are usually preserved while the remains of land animals and plants are often only preserved if they have been washed into the deposits. As a result, aquatic animals are well represented as fossils while land animals are much rarer. The most important fossil-bearing rocks are limestone, sandstone, shale and chalk.

Types of fossils

The heavily mineralized hard parts of animals such as their shells, tests, bones or teeth may be preserved unchanged as fossils. The occurrence of unchanged fossils increases in progressively younger deposits and many Pliocene and Pleistocene fossils consist mainly of the original hard tissues of the organism.

Many fossils consist of the original hard parts of the animal or plant with minerals from the surrounding rocks added. These minerals enter in solution and impregnate the tissues, increasing their hardness and weight but preserving their structure. This process is known as **petrifaction**. Alternatively the original tissues may be dissolved away and replaced by minerals entering from the surrounding rocks. This process is known as **replacement** and if it occurs gradually or molecule by molecule, the structure of the fossilized tissues will be preserved. On the other hand, if the hard parts are dissolved away rapidly, a cavity will be left in the consolidated sediments. This cavity may later become filled with minerals and a **mould** will result. An internal mould represents the filling of the original shell or test, while an external mould shows the original appearance of the organism. In both cases the internal structure will have been lost.

Parts of an organism lacking hard parts are sometimes preserved in special conditions in which all but the carbon content of the original tissues is lost. This usually results in the preservation of a film of carbon lying along the bedding plane of a sedimentary rock and demonstrates the appearance of the original organism. This process is known as **carbonization** and fossil plants and graptolites are often preserved in this way.

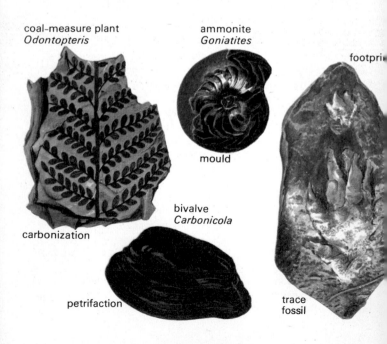

coal-measure plant
Odontopteris

ammonite
Goniatites

footpri

mould

carbonization

bivalve
Carbonicola

petrifaction

trace
fossil

Starunia rhinoceros

Fossils consist of any trace of past life; they may therefore be simply the footprints, burrow or borings of animals, or even the fossilized droppings (coprolites) of animals. These are known as **trace fossils**.

Some of the most spectacular fossils result from preservation in special conditions. For example, amber is fossil resin and occurs in deposits around the Baltic Sea. When the deposits of amber were accumulating, insects and spiders occasionally became trapped in the sticky resin and their complete bodies and even colours have been preserved for millions of years. Occasionally organisms may be trapped in volcanic ash and in this situation the impressions of the soft parts may be preserved. This sometimes also happens in very fine sediments where even fossilized jellyfish are known. In the northern parts of Asia and North America the soil has been permanently frozen for several thousand years and complete mammoths, rhinoceroses and other mammals have been discovered preserved in these frozen deposits. These remains are so well preserved that even the stomach contents and food in the mouth can be studied. Remains may also be preserved by natural pickling. At Starunia in Poland a complete rhinoceros was discovered pickled in a mixture of brine and tar. This specimen was over 10 000 years old but again it was so well preserved that its stomach contents could be studied.

What fossils can tell us

The study of living organisms tells us much of what we know about the animals and plants that inhabit our planet but a knowledge of fossils introduces the time element into these studies and in so doing reveals the effects that long-term changes may have.

Evolution

The process of natural selection operates on small differences that exist between living things. If an animal possesses a new feature or a slight modification of an existing feature that enables it to live more efficiently than its contemporaries, then that animal is more likely to survive and will probably leave more offspring than its fellows. As a result of heredity it is likely that these descendants will resemble their parents and will therefore have more offspring and so on until the new feature is present throughout the population. As a result of natural selection animals and plants change through time and new kinds of organisms may develop. The process by which existing organisms change and new kinds of organisms arise is known as evolution. The theory of evolution was formulated by the British biologist Charles Darwin and was first published in his book *The Origin of Species,* 1859. Charles Darwin was an outstanding zoologist who also worked with fossils and his experience with fossil groups certainly influenced his ideas as he developed his theory.

As evolution works on very small differences between organisms the changes that it produces occur very slowly over long periods of time. With the study of fossils, however, marked evolutionary changes can be demonstrated. For example, over the last fifty million years the one-toed foot of the modern horse has evolved from the three- or four-toed foot of the tiny Eocene horse *Hyracotherium* and at the same time horses have increased from the size of a terrier dog to their present size. The relative size and complexity of the brain of the horse also increased. Other important evolutionary changes occurred at the same time during the history of the horse and these involved their teeth, and skulls. The occurrence of these evolutionary changes may have been suspected from the study of living horses and their relatives, the rhinoceroses and tapirs, but they can only be demonstrated by a study of the relevant fossils.

Relationships

Living animals and plants have resulted from the evolution of organisms since the origin of life and the study of fossils may

Changes in the ancestry of the horse as revealed by fossils.

four-toed foot

Hyracotherium Palaeocene – Eocene

three-toed foot

Miohippus Oligocene

one-toed foot

Equus Recent

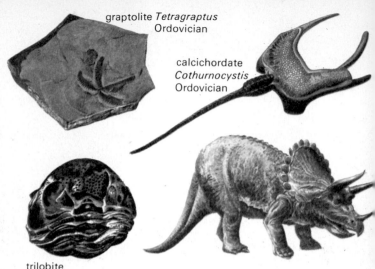

graptolite *Tetragraptus*
Ordovician

calcichordate
Cothurnocystis
Ordovician

trilobite
Phacops Silurian – Devonian   dinosaur *Triceratops* Cretaceous

reveal the ancestors and relationships of groups of organisms. Perhaps the best ancestral form that has been discovered as a fossil is *Archaeopteryx* (p.90) from the Jurassic of Bavaria. *Archaeopteryx* has feathers and is therefore definitely a bird, but it also has many features of its skeleton that indicate a close relationship to the reptiles and in particular to the dinosaurs and early crocodiles. The study of relationships is based upon detailed study of living forms. Evidence from living animals suggests that the phylum Chordata (p.79), which includes the vertebrates, is related to the Echinodermata (p.72), which includes the starfishes and sea urchins. Detailed study of an obscure Ordovician group of fossils, the Calcichordata, has demonstrated that these two living phyla are indeed related.

Extinct animals

Before the nineteenth century it was believed that all species of living things were created in their present form and that no other species had ever existed. The study of fossils during the last century effectively destroyed this belief by demonstrating the remains of numerous extinct animals and plants whose existence would not have been suspected from the study of living organisms. Without fossils the existence of graptolites (p.44), ammonites (p.50) or trilobites (p.66) would never have been suspected and even the wildest imagination would not have suggested animals as bizarre as the dinosaurs or pterosaurs.

Distribution

The present distribution of animals and plants may be more clearly understood from the study of fossils. For example, tapirs occur in the jungles of south-east Asia and in South America but under present conditions it is very unlikely that they could have migrated from one region to the other. Study of the fossils, however, demonstrates that several million years ago tapirs were common in North America and Eurasia, even occurring in Europe in the Pliocene. Therefore, the present distribution of these mammals merely reflects their survival in two areas of their former wide distribution. Similarly camels occur in Asia and Africa while their only close relatives – the llamas – are known only from South America. Fossils, however, demonstrate that for the last thirty million years camels were very common in North America and from there they spread to South America and Asia, while they only became extinct in North America a few thousand years ago.

distribution of tapirs
recent distribution
fossil distribution

Development of animal structures

The study of fossils demonstrates stages in the evolution of numerous complex structures in living organisms. For example, the front leg of a mammal consists of numerous small and several larger bones. The arrangement and position of these bones can be understood by a study of the limbs of early reptiles and the fins of fossil fishes which show the stages through which the bones evolved from the fin to the fully developed mammalian limb.

Past climates

The past two million years have seen great climatic changes that are demonstrated by fossils. At least three times, ice sheets swept southwards from the Arctic to cover Britain and the rest of Europe as far south as London, while so much water was locked up in the ice that sea levels dropped and the English Channel and parts of the North Sea were dry land. Similarly during the Eocene Period about fifty million years ago the area around London and Paris enjoyed tropical conditions and fossil plants from the Isle of Sheppey indicate the presence of jungles similar to those of modern Malaya.

Fore-limb bones in a fish, reptile and mammal. Changes in the shape and relative size of different bones reflect changes in methods of locomotion. **Key: a** scapula, **b** humerus, **c** radius, **d** ulna.

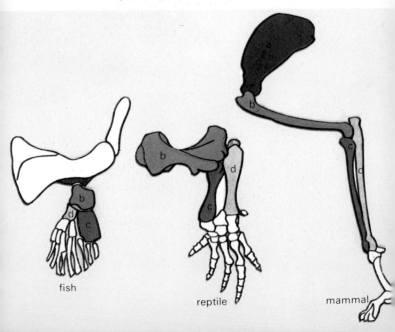

fish

reptile

mammal

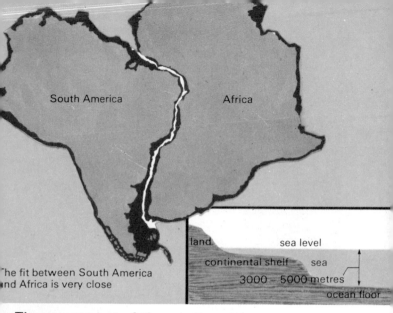

South America

Africa

The fit between South America and Africa is very close

land   sea level

continental shelf   sea

3000 – 5000 metres

ocean floor

The movement of the continents

If you take a map of the world and cut out the continents then their shapes can be fitted together. This agreement in shape was commented on by Sir Francis Bacon as long ago as 1620 and from the seventeenth to nineteenth centuries it was thought that the Atlantic had developed when the Americas and Europe moved apart as a result of the biblical Flood. However, the idea that the continents have indeed drifted apart, or the 'Theory of Continental Displacement' as it is called, has only become accepted by the scientific world during the last twenty-five years.

The shape of each continent includes not only the land area but also the floor of the shallow epicontinental, or shelf seas, which extend as far as the edge of the continental shelf. This is the region where the seabed falls away with depths increasing rapidly from that of the shallow shelf seas to the 5 000–8 000 metre depths that are typical of the oceans. If the shapes of the continental shelf are included in our jigsaw then the fit between the continents is very close indeed.

It is thought that the continents of the world originally fitted together as a single land mass called Pangaea and that they remained joined until Mesozoic times. During middle Mesozoic times, however, this supercontinent split into northern and southern parts

15

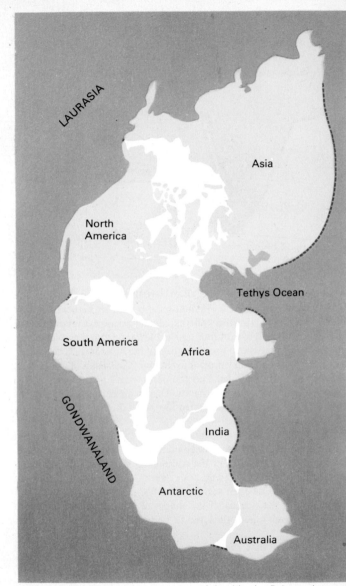

The continents as they may have been joined in the Palaeozoic.

known as Laurasia and Gondwanaland respectively. These were separated by an ocean known as Tethys of which the Mediterranean is a remnant. In Cretaceous times North America and Europe began to separate and a narrow North Atlantic Ocean existed at the start of the Caenozoic. The Atlantic has since expanded to its present size and is still widening at the rate of almost two and a half centimetres per year.

The mechanism by which the continents are moved is not known but several lines of evidence are used to interpret the movement and to establish the position of the continents at different times in the past.

The Scottish mountains

The Palaeozoic rocks that form the Caledonian Mountains are part of a greater mountain system also found in Greenland, Scandinavia and North America. Geological evidence indicates that these rocks originally formed a continuous mountain chain but with the contin-

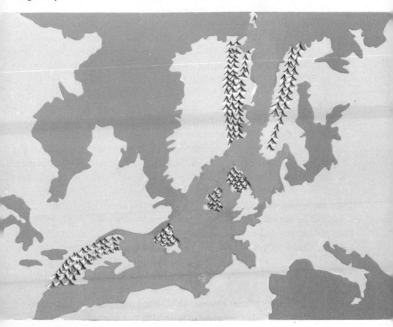

Mountains in Europe and North America probably formed a single continuous range before the formation of the Atlantic.

ents in their present positions, several thousand kilometres of this mountain chain would need to have been eroded away. It is more likely that parts of this mountain system were once joined and have become separated as the continents moved apart and the Atlantic formed.

Past climates

Fossil evidence of past climates indicates that the world's climatic belts once had very different distributions relative to the continents and these differences may indicate that the continents themselves have moved. For example, 250–300 million years ago parts of the southern land masses were under a large ice sheet and material from the ice was deposited over a wide area. The direction of movement of the ice has been established and indicates that the same ice sheet flowed from Africa into South America where it deposited rocks of African origin. This could only have happened if the two continents were in contact. This and other evidence indicates that a super-continent existed near the South Pole.

About 300 million years ago parts of the northern continents experienced tropical conditions in which the coal forests flourished. This suggests that these regions were near the equator and, as the animals and plants are similar throughout the coal deposits, it also suggests that they lived on a single land mass.

The Earth's magnetism

The ancient magnetism of the Earth (palaeomagnetism) is studied in rocks containing iron minerals. When igneous rocks cool at the surface their contained iron molecules become magnetized in the Earth's magnetic field and are orientated to agree with the position of the magnetic poles. When the rocks solidify the molecules are fixed and thus record the position of the poles at that time. A similar thing occurs as some sedimentary rocks are formed. The latitude at which the rocks form is indicated by the angle of dip of the molecules and their longitude is shown by the orientation of the molecules. Study of palaeomagnetism in rocks between 100 and 300 million years old from North America and Europe suggests the existence of two like magnetic poles which is impossible. However, the distance between these poles is related to the width of the North Atlantic and it therefore appears that when the rocks were formed on the two continents the North Atlantic did not exist. This and similar palaeomagnetic evidence from other continents is used to plot the movement of the land masses.

The ocean floor

Recent studies of the ocean floor have demonstrated that a series of high ridges extends down the mid-Atlantic, around the southern tip of Africa, gives off a branch up the Gulf of Aden and runs between Antarctica and Australia before turning northwards to run up the eastern Pacific. In the Atlantic these ridges include a central rift valley over 2 000 metres deep. Parts of the ridges are displaced by fractures that are often hundreds of kilometres long and the majority of oceanic earthquakes occur at the fractures, which in itself indicates movement of the earth's crust in these regions. Study of the ocean

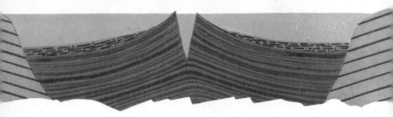

Cross-section of ocean floor showing mid-oceanic rise and trench.

floor to the east and west of the ridge demonstrates that new ocean floor is produced in the valley and is spreading outwards from the ridge. It also demonstrates that the age of the ocean floor rocks increases progressively away from the ridge and that the oldest rocks of the North Atlantic floor are only about eighty million years old. However, these rocks are not very close to the edge of the continental shelf and the Atlantic probably began to form in Jurassic times about 180 million years ago.

Distribution of animals and plants

The study of the past and present distribution of organisms provides numerous examples of animals or plants that only occur in regions now separated by wide stretches of ocean and which are unknown in the intervening areas (note: this, therefore, excludes patterns of distribution discussed on page 13). For example, the ancestor of the horse, *Hyracotherium,* is known from the Palaeocene and Eocene of North America and from Lower Eocene rocks near London but is unknown from Asia. It is therefore likely that there was a land connection across the North Atlantic in early Eocene times which in turn suggests that the Atlantic was much narrower than it is now.

Hyracotherium is known from the Upper Palaeocene of North America and the Eocene of Europe and North America. This suggests that it migrated across the North Atlantic when it was much narrower than it is today.

Similarly the Permian reptile *Mesosaurus* is known from Brazil and parts of Africa but is unknown from the numerous faunas of Permian reptiles elsewhere in the world. It is very unlikely that *Mesosaurus* could have swum between the two regions and this suggests that in Permian times it was able to travel freely from one continent to the other, which would only have been possible if the two continents were very close together.

We have seen that several independent lines of evidence support the theory that the continents have changed their positions during the last 200–300 million years to reach their present positions.

The economic uses of fossils

Fossils are very important in geology and in much geological work they are used simply as markers which indicate the age of the rocks in which they occur. When sedimentary rocks are deposited, the oldest are at the bottom and the layers of rock become progressively younger as we move up the sequence. Unfortunately this initially simple situation may become very complicated as a result of different rates of deposition or total breaks in deposition, erosion of the surface or folding and faulting of the rocks. When fossils are included in sedimentary rocks they enable the geologist to work out the correct sequence of the rock layers or **strata**. Fossils used in this sort of work must be relatively common, must change rapidly with time and the species should have wide geographical distributions. Some good **zone fossils** are the ammonites, forams, ostracods and trilobites. As we saw on page 10, animal and plant species change as a result of evolution but the species to which any individual organism or fossil belongs is fixed and cannot change no matter how much the rock that contains it may be faulted, eroded or inverted.

To work out the correct sequence of strata in an area, the stratigrapher makes a study of the fossils from an undisturbed unit of rock and from this he will learn the order in which the fossil species occur. He may also learn the relative abundance of different species

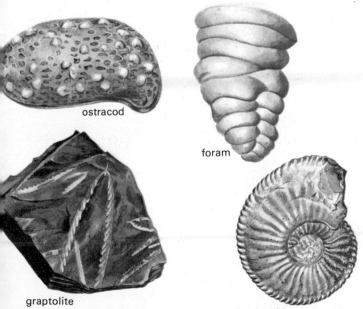

ostracod

foram

graptolite
Didymograptus Ordovician

ammonite *Amaltheus* Jurassic

at each level. For example, let us say that of three species of ammonites **a**, **b** and **c**, **a** is the oldest and **c** the youngest. Then in an undisturbed rock sequence **a**, **b** and **c** will occur as shown in the figure. If the species are found in the order **c**, **b**, **a**, then the stratigrapher will know that the rocks have been turned over or inverted. On the other hand if only **a** and **c** are found in some areas then he will know that deposition was not occurring during the time that species **b** was in existence or that conditions were unsuitable for the survival of species **b**. Of course the stratigrapher works with many species and often he studies differences in abundance between species rather than changes in species. For example, if he finds that in one rock 60% of the forams belong to species **d** and 40% to species **e** while in a later rock 80% belong to **e** and only 20% to **d** then he will be able to identify these rocks wherever they occur with these species included in sufficient numbers for large samples to be collected. This sort of work, known as **correlation**, is a very important use of fossils and has great economic application.

Fossils are used extensively in exploration and in the exploitation of mineral resources. Deposits of minerals often occur in rocks of the same age over wide areas. For example, almost all coal occurs in rocks of Carboniferous age and most of the oil in the North Sea is in

Folded rocks showing fossils used to assess sequence.

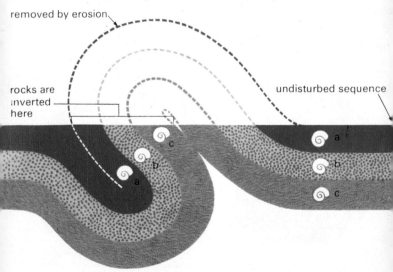

removed by erosion

rocks are inverted here

undisturbed sequence

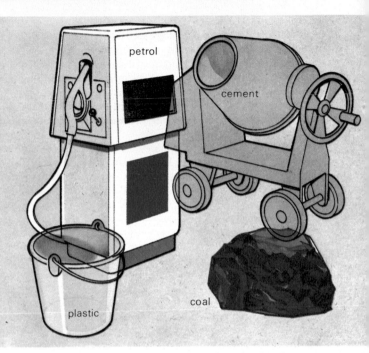

Some fossil fuels and everyday things produced from them.

Jurassic rocks. It is therefore important to be able to identify rocks of different ages with considerable accuracy. In drilling for oil, cores or columns of rock are removed from the borehole at regular intervals and the study of the fossils – usually forams and ostracods – included in these cores enables the geologist to establish the age of rock through which the drill is passing. This is important as drilling will continue if the borehole has not yet reached the potentially productive zone and likewise it can be ended if this zone has been passed.

Many fossils are themselves important economically, for example, coal, oil and natural gas are known as 'fossil fuels' as their deposits have resulted from organic activity in the past. Coal is used not only as a fuel but also in cosmetics, tar, saccharine and drugs, while oil is used for a host of fuels as well as plastics, fertilizers and in animal food. Limestone consists mainly of the remains of marine organisms and is used extensively in building.

The age of rocks

Until recently the study of geology used a time-scale that was based on the occurrence of events during the history of the Earth. It was important to know the order in which events in a sequence occurred but it was, and still is, less important to know exactly how many years elapsed between events or how long ago they occurred. As a result, a relative time-scale was developed from the study of rocks and fossils with divisions marking the incidence of important and widespread geological changes.

Throughout the history of geology, however, attempts have been made to estimate the age of the Earth and its different rocks. Theories using the Bible, rate of cooling of the Earth, salt content of the oceans and several other lines of 'evidence' have resulted in estimates of the Earth's age ranging from about 4 000 years to several thousand million years.

Until recently studies of the rate of deposition of sediments gave the most reliable geological estimates of the age in years or absolute age of the different rocks. Sedimentary rocks have been deposited constantly since the cooling of the Earth's crust but no one area contains deposits representing all stages of geological time. It is therefore necessary to study rocks from many different parts of the world. Several estimates have been made of the total thickness of rocks that have been deposited since the beginning of the Cambrian with the highest and most recent being a figure of almost 150 000 metres. Rocks are usually deposited in areas where the seabed is sinking gradually and the rate of deposition is related to the rate of subsidence. The rate of deposition is also influenced by the amount of sediment carried to the area of deposition and the deposits are influenced by erosion of their surface. Estimates of absolute ages based on the thickness of deposits assume regular growth in thickness and that rocks of all ages are included. In 1959 Sir Arthur Holmes published the results of detailed work that gave absolute ages from the beginning of the Cambrian. These estimates agree fairly closely with those obtained by methods of dating using radioactive decay.

Radioactive dating of rocks

The atoms of every element consist of a nucleus that is made up of particles known as protons and neutrons, while particles known as electrons orbit around the nucleus. The number of protons and electrons in the atom controls the properties of the element and is always constant for each element. The atomic number of an element is the number of protons in the nucleus of each atom. The atomic mass of an element is the total number of protons and neutrons in the nucleus.

The nuclei of radioactive elements tend to change spontaneously. The original nucleus is known as the 'parent' and the resultant nuclei are known as the 'daughters'. The time taken for half the parent nuclei in a sample of an element to change is known as the half life and is constant for the element studied and independent of the sample size. Isotopes are forms of an element that cannot be distinguished chemically but which differ in the number of neutrons in their nuclei. Thus the isotopes of an element agree in atomic number but differ in their atomic masses. For example, uranium has the chemical symbol 'U' and the isotopes U^{238} and U^{235} have atomic masses 238 and 235 respectively but both have the atomic number 92. The half life of the series by which U^{238} changes to lead Pb^{206} is 4 510 million years while that in which U^{235} changes to Pb^{207} is 713 million years.

Igneous rocks are formed by the cooling of molten rock. When these igneous rocks or volcanic lava solidify, small amounts of radioactive elements may be trapped. Thus the amount of the radioactive element included is fixed when the rock forms. This element will decay and the product of decay will be trapped in the rock. Therefore if a sample of the rock is taken it may be possible to discover the ratio of the original parent to the new daughters and if the half life for the series is known then the age of the rock may be calculated.

For dating by this method radioactive minerals must be present, the rocks must be unaltered by events after their formation, and the breakdown sequence and half life must be known. Several series of radioactive breakdown are used for dating rocks of Palaeozoic, Mesozoic and Caenozoic age. These include the rubidium: strontium method and the potassium: argon method. In the potassium: argon (K/Ar) method, the potassium isotope K^{40} breaks down to the argon isotope Ar^{40} and this sequence has a half life of 1 270 million years which means that it is particularly useful for dating Mesozoic and Caenozoic rocks.

Radioactive methods of dating are still being perfected but they allow the geologist to discover fairly accurate absolute ages for rocks by a method that is not influenced by changes in deposition or climate etc. Unfortunately many rocks cannot be dated by these methods and therefore the classical comparative methods are still of great importance.

species:
Felis silvestris genus: *Felis* family: Felidae order:
Carnivora

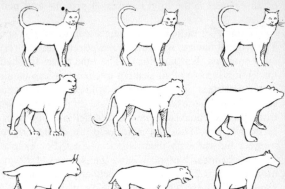

Scientific names

Animals and plants are divided into several groupings that are used by scientists. A **species** is a group of organisms in which the members have the potential to breed together and produce fertile offspring. The members of one species cannot breed successfully with members of another species. In a few cases the boundaries between two species may appear blurred; for example, the horse and donkey belong to different species but they may breed together to produce mules. The mule, however, is not fertile and therefore the horse and donkey are correctly placed in separate species. The scientific name for a species consists of two Latin or Latinized words that are always printed in italics and should be underlined when written. The scientific name for the horse is *Equus caballus* and the name for the wild cat is *Felis silvestris*. The second part of each name defines the species and is called the **specific** or **trivial** name; it always begins with a small letter and is meaningless if used alone. Similar or closely related species are grouped to form a **genus** (plural genera) and the first part of the species name which refers to the genus is called the **generic** name. It always begins with a capital letter and may be used alone. For example, the genus *Equus* (horses) includes the species *Equus caballus* (horse), *Equus asinus* (ass or donkey) and *Equus burchelli* (zebra).

Closely related genera are grouped into **families**. The family name always ends with the letters 'ae' and members of the same family usually resemble each other in appearance. Families are grouped into **orders** with organisms that are less closely related. For example, the horses, tapirs and rhinoceroses are grouped in the order Perissodactyla while the apes, monkeys, man and the lemurs are grouped in the order Primates. Orders are themselves grouped into **classes** and the members of different classes differ from each other in important features of organization. Some familiar classes are: the Mammalia (mammals), Reptilia (reptiles), Aves (birds) and Pisces (fishes). Classes are grouped into **phyla** (singular: phylum) and members of different phyla differ in fundamental features of organization such as body support and methods of locomotion. For example, members of the phylum Chordata all have an internal rod or notochord at some stage in their development. This stiffens the body and allows them to swim. Members of the phylum Arthropoda (insects, crabs, lobsters etc.) all have hard outer skeletons and jointed limbs. Phyla are grouped into **kingdoms**. The kingdom Animalia includes all the animals and the kingdom Plantae includes the plants.

chordate

invertebrate

plant

The groups of fossils

In this book the fossils are treated in three main sections: invertebrates, chordates and plants. The invertebrates are those animals that lack an internal bony skeleton. This is an artificial grouping that includes over twenty distinct phyla with animals ranging from the single-celled protozoa to the insects, squids and starfishes, and comprising over ninety-five per cent of all animals. The majority of important fossils are invertebrates with the molluscs (p.45) as the most important larger forms or **macrofossils**, and the forams (p.36) and ostracods (p.71) as important small forms or **microfossils**.

The vertebrates form a subphylum of the Chordata (p.79). Members of this group are characterized by the possession of an internal skeleton composed of bone or cartilage, and in particular by the presence of a backbone or vertebral column. Fossil vertebrates are less common than invertebrates but in museums they usually receive detailed treatment, frequently with spectacular displays of dinosaurs and large mammals.

Fossil plants (kingdom Plantae) are particularly common in deposits of Carboniferous age in which their accumulated remains form coal. Fossil leaves and fruit may be locally abundant and in some areas fossil wood is frequently encountered. In general, however, fossil plants are rarer than fossil invertebrates.

The Precambrian

Precambrian times cover about 3 000 million years and ended about 600 million years ago with the start of the Cambrian. Fossils are very rare in Precambrian rocks and when they do occur their interpretation is often difficult as the rocks have frequently been altered by geological processes. Blue-green algae are among the simplest living organisms. They are minute, single-celled plants and they occur as fossils in rocks from Swaziland that are about 3 200 million years old. The most common Precambrian fossils belong to the group known as stromatolites. These are often large, calcareous masses that have a layered structure. Stromatolites have survived to the present day and they are known to be associations of different kinds of organisms including blue-green algae.

Rocks about 1 900 million years old from Ontario, Canada contain stromatolites as well as fossil fungi and bacteria. The oldest fossil remains that can be definitely identified as animals occur in rocks from Africa that are about 2 000 million years old, while sponge spicules (p.38) and jellyfish are known from Australia in rocks that are 1 500 million years old.

Rocks in Charnwood Forest, Leicestershire, England are about 690 million years old and contain the remains of *Charnia* which may be an early kind of seaweed or may be a coelenterate. The Australian Precambrian fossil *Spriggina* is worm-like in appearance and may be related to the ancestry of the worms and arthropods.

Spriggina

Charnia

The Palaeozoic

Marine invertebrates and plants were well established before the start of Palaeozoic times and echinoderms, annelids, graptolites, bryozoans, brachiopods, molluscs and sponges occur in Cambrian rocks, while about half the known Cambrian fossils are trilobites with over 1 000 species represented. During Ordovician times the invertebrates increased in abundance and diversity. The Cambrian graptolites were all net-like forms similar to *Dictyonema* but during Ordovician times branched forms such as *Didymograptus* became very abundant. Trilobites remained common but the brachiopods were the commonest invertebrates in shallow seas and are represented

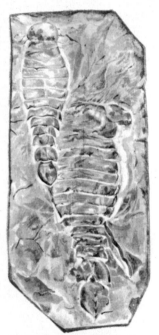

trilobite *Calymene*
Silurian – Devonian

eurypterids (large, aquatic arthropods) *Pterygotus*
Ordovician – Devonian

reptile *Dimetrodon* Permian

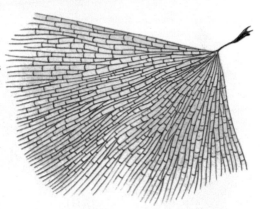

net-like
graptolite
Dictyonema
Cambrian —
Carboniferous

by forms such as *Strophomena*. The rest of the Palaeozoic saw the rise of the ammonites, bivalve molluscs, gastropods, crinoids and several other groups. Towards the end of the era characteristic Palaeozoic groups, such as the trilobites, graptolites, many sea lilies and rugose corals became extinct.

Land invertebrates first occur in the Devonian and the remains of millipedes, mites, spiders, wingless insects and crustaceans similar to woodlice are known. In Carboniferous times the coal forests supported a well-developed invertebrate fauna with snails, millipedes, centipedes, scorpions and flying insects well represented.

Vertebrates first occur in the Ordovician and were well established by Devonian times, with well-known forms such as *Pteraspis* and *Cephalaspis* representing the armoured fishes. Bony fishes became common in the Devonian and some forms such as *Eusthenopteron* had lungs and limb-like fins and could 'walk' on land. Amphibians had evolved by the end of Devonian times and expanded rapidly in the Carboniferous with some coal-forest forms reaching five metres in length. The earliest reptiles occurred in late Carboniferous times and during the Permian the reptiles became very important. The lizard-like *Dimetrodon* was a carnivore, about three metres long.

Fossil marine algae are known throughout the Palaeozoic but the first land plants occur in Upper Silurian rocks from Australia. Land plants expanded rapidly and Lower Devonian rocks from Rhynie near Aberdeen contain fossil peat with the preserved roots, stems and spores of well-developed land plants. Ferns, horsetails and seed ferns are known from Upper Devonian rocks and during Carboniferous times a flourishing land flora produced the coal deposits.

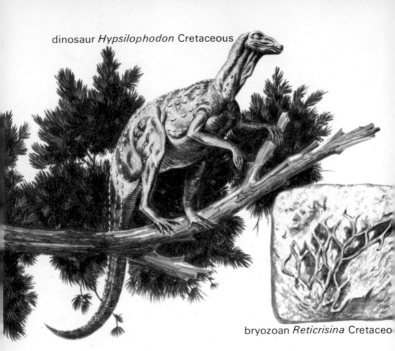

dinosaur *Hypsilophodon* Cretaceous

bryozoan *Reticrisina* Cretaceo

The Mesozoic

Several new groups of marine invertebrates appeared in early Mesozoic times. The rugose corals were replaced by the scleractine corals
which survive as an important group. The Palaeozoic brachiopod
groups had largely declined but the rhynchonellids and terebratulids
became important. The greatest changes occurred, however, among
the molluscs which radiated widely to become by far the commonest
of the larger marine invertebrates with the ammonites, belemnites
and gastropods as very important groups. There was also a great
expansion of the bivalve molluscs with the appearance of the oysters
in Triassic times. The first lobster-like crustaceans also appeared in
Triassic times to be followed in Jurassic times by the first crabs. The
chalk of Europe is of Cretaceous age and in this period the most
important order of bryozoans first appears.

Marine vertebrates included the sharks, rays and bony fishes which
were common and were developing towards their modern forms.
Marine reptiles were also very important and probably had ways of
life similar to the living whales and seals. The ichthyosaurs were

fully adapted to marine life while the plesiosaurs, mosasaurs and turtles were common and varied.

On land great changes occurred in the animal and plant life. Ferns and conifers were common while maidenhair trees were abundant and some cycads were developing flower-like cones. True flowering plants only appeared in middle Cretaceous times but before the end of that period the development of a modern type of flora was well advanced with fig, poplar, magnolia and plane represented. Land invertebrates were also approaching their modern form and the expansion of the more advanced plants was followed by a great increase in the flying insects such as beetles, flies, butterflies and bees.

The expansion of the insects was followed by a wide radiation of the small, insect-eating Mesozoic mammals. The Mesozoic is, however, best known as the 'Age of Reptiles'. Mammal-like reptiles were important in Triassic times and at the end of that period the mammals arose. During Jurassic and Cretaceous times the dinosaurs were by far the most important land vertebrates while in Jurassic times the vertebrates first took to the air with the development of numerous flying reptiles and the birds.

At the end of the Cretaceous a wave of extinctions occurred. In the seas the ammonites and many marine reptiles became extinct while on land the extinction of the dinosaurs and flying reptiles left the way open for the expansion of the birds and mammals and the development of the modern fauna.

ammonite
Promicroceras Jurassic

cone *Araucaria* Cretaceous

The Caenozoic

The marine invertebrates of early Caenozoic times were essentially modern in character. Large foraminiferans known as *Nummulites* were common and survived until Oligocene times. A few belemnites survived into the Palaeocene but the most important Caenozoic cephalopods were the squids and cuttlefish. Bivalves and gastropods

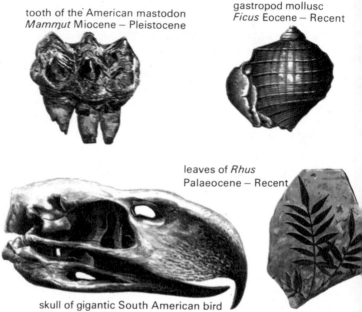

tooth of the American mastodon
Mammut Miocene – Pleistocene

gastropod mollusc
Ficus Eocene – Recent

leaves of *Rhus*
Palaeocene – Recent

skull of gigantic South American bird
Phororhacos Miocene

were very abundant and the presence of *Conus* and *Ficus* in the European middle Caenozoic faunas suggests the existence of warm-water conditions. By Pliocene times many modern genera had evolved but species now extinct were still abundant. At this time large coral reefs occupied much of southern Britain and their presence resulted in the formation of the Coralline Crag deposits of East Anglia. The Caenozoic also saw the development of the modern fauna of bony fishes and the Eocene fish faunas of Europe were almost modern in aspect. Sharks and rays were also abundant and generally modern but an extinct species of *Carcharodon* from the British Pliocene was a huge shark about twenty metres long. Whales first appeared in the Eocene and rapidly became important throughout the world. Early whales such as *Dorudon* had serrated teeth and some attained a large size. An interesting new group was the Sirenia or sea cows which arose in the Eocene. These fully aquatic, plant-eating mammals were very successful throughout the Caenozoic and are today represented by the dugong and manatee.

On land the evolution of flowering plants continued rapidly. Eocene floras of the London area included numerous palms and other tropical elements while temperate floras extended as far north as Greenland. Grasslands probably first developed in the Oligocene and in late Miocene and Pliocene times a huge belt of grassland stretched from China to western Europe and north Africa.

The mammals were dominant on land and became very diverse during the Caenozoic. The modern continents had become completely separated and on many of them different groups of mammals were evolving independently. In Australia the marsupials were dominant and a large fauna of mammals evolved without any familiar forms being represented. Part of this fauna survives today and it includes the kangaroos, wombats, and koalas. South America was also an island continent for most of the Caenozoic and many bizarre mammals evolved there. Marsupials were the dominant flesh-eating animals, but they shared this way of life with huge birds. In late Caenozoic times the Central American region became land for the first time and northern mammals were able to invade South America.

In Palaeocene and Eocene times, bizarre, large, plant-eating mammals such as *Coryphodon* were common while the Oligocene fauna of Asia included *Paraceratherium* (also known as *Baluchitherium*) which is the largest-known land mammal and stood about six metres at the shoulder. The birds were also important and evolved rapidly. Some birds such as the penguins became marine, while a host were able to fly. Some, however, were flightless, running forms such as the ostrich and the South American Miocene *Phororhacos* which was a flesh-eating bird with a huge beak and a skull over forty centimetres long.

Late Caenozoic times are marked by the Pleistocene Ice Ages and the rise of man. The Ice Ages had a profound effect on marine and land life especially in the Northern Hemisphere and a wave of extinctions affecting the large Pleistocene mammals resulted in the development of the modern fauna, while the influence of man has been increasingly important especially over the last 1 000 years.

FOSSIL INVERTEBRATES

Protozoa

The phylum Protozoa includes the single-celled organisms that are the simplest-known animals. The amoeba *Paramecium*, and *Euglena* are familiar protozoans and most members of the phylum are very small, rarely exceeding a few millimetres in diameter.

Foraminifera

The order Foraminifera (forams for short) includes mainly marine protozoans that are important as fossils in Mesozoic and Caenozoic rocks and their importance has greatly increased as the study of rock cores produced in exploratory drilling has become widely used in the search for minerals (p.21).

The majority of forams have calcareous, many chambered shells or tests, that have a wide variety of shapes in the different species. The shells carry numerous perforations through which pass processes of the soft tissue. Other forams have tests consisting of sand grains or other small particles that are stuck together. Alternatively the test may consist of an organic substance known as chitin which is similar in composition to the outer skeleton of the insects.

Forams range from the Ordovician to Recent and they are very

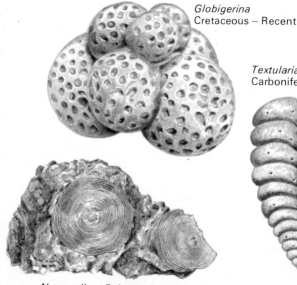

Globigerina
Cretaceous – Recent

Textularia
Carboniferous – Recent

Nummulites Palaeocene – Oligocene

abundant in Upper Mesozoic and Caenozoic rocks. During early Caenozoic (Palaeocene–Oligocene) times forams known as *Nummulites* were abundant. These are shaped like coins and some are several centimetres in diameter. *Nummulites* is especially abundant in the Eocene and Oligocene beds of south-eastern Britain and in the Mediterranean area.

Radiolarians

Members of the order Radiolaria are entirely marine and mainly planktonic. They are less important than forams as fossils but over 800 genera are known and radiolarians may be extremely abundant in some deposits where their accumulated remains form 'radiolarian oozes' which only accumulate at depths exceeding 4 500 metres. The radiolarian shell is usually composed of silica, though some species have shells of strontium sulphate. The shell may take a variety of forms and some are a few millimetres in diameter while some colonial radiolarians may be a few centimetres across. Radiolarians range from rocks of Precambrian to Recent age and their classification is based on details of the shell including the arrangement of spines and perforations and the pattern of the skeleton. Forams and radiolarians are usually collected by special sieving techniques and are studied at high magnifications.

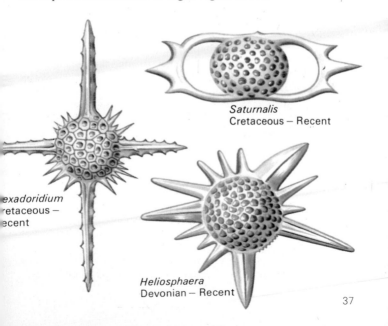

Saturnalis
Cretaceous – Recent

exadoridium
retaceous –
ecent

Heliosphaera
Devonian – Recent

37

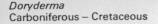

Doryderma
Carboniferous – Cretaceous

Ventriculites
Cretaceous

Hydnoceras
Devonian – Carboniferous

Sponges

Sponges are the simplest multicellular animals. They feed by extracting food particles from a stream of water that is drawn in through pores in the sides of the body and which leaves through a large opening or cloaca.

Many sponges have an internal skeleton consisting of silica or calcite and it is only sponges with such a structure that are important as fossils. The calcite or silica is formed into elements known as **spicules** that are scattered through the soft tissues of the sponge or joined to form a rigid skeleton. Isolated spicules occur as fossils but are difficult to collect and identify, whereas those sponges with rigid skeletons are often preserved as large fossils with characteristic shapes. Sponges having silica spicules range from the Precambrian while those having calcareous skeletons first occur in the Devonian.

Siliceous sponges are grouped into the classes Hyalospongea and Demospongea. Hyalosponges are long and thin, or like elongated funnels. They are common in Mesozoic rocks and *Ventriculites* is a typical member of this group. Hyalosponges are characterized by their spicules which have three growth axes at right angles to one another, whereas in the demosponges this spicule form does not occur. Calcareous sponges may resemble siliceous sponges in their growth forms but usually have thicker walls and less regular shapes.

Corals

Corals are members of the phylum Coelenterata which also includes the jellyfishes and sea anemones. They are first recorded from the Lower Ordovician and are still an important marine group. As they have calcareous skeletons the corals are frequently fossilized but they have evolved only slowly and therefore are not particularly useful in stratigraphy.

Several features of corals are important for their identification and classification. They may be **colonial** – that is, consisting of many joined individuals – or they may be **solitary** and consist of only a single individual. They may grow to form clumps, in which case they are said to have a **massive** growth form, they may be **branching** or they may be **encrusting** and grow like moss on other objects. Each individual of a colony or each solitary individual is called a **corallite** and each complete group is a **corallum**. In life each corallite houses the soft parts of the animal that are known as **polyps**. These soft parts are supported by plates or divisions inside the corallite and

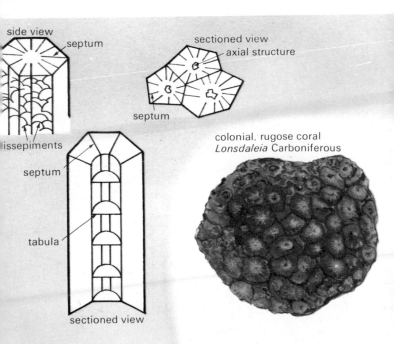

side view
septum
sectioned view
axial structure
septum
dissepiments
septum
tabula
sectioned view

colonial, rugose coral
Lonsdaleia Carboniferous

the type and arrangement of these plates is important. Major vertical plates or **septa** usually divide the corallite and appear as lines in cross-section. Between the septa there may be smaller divisions termed **dissepiments**. These are usually most abundant near the outer parts of the corallite and may have any orientation from nearly vertical to nearly horizontal. The centre of the corallite often differs from the rest in appearance and this region is termed the **axial structure**. It may consist of a vertical, rod-like process or may have a diffuse, sponge-like texture. Major horizontal plates or **tabulae** may also occur and these are most important in the axial region.

Corals are usually indentified from study of polished or thin sections. Important features are the growth form, arrangement of the septae, tabulae, dissepiments and axial structure.

Tabulate corals

The subclass Tabulata is an extinct group of corals that were the first to appear in the fossil record. Tabulate corals range from the

tabulate coral
Favosites
Silurian – Devonian
tabulae are
shown in rows
up each corallite

tabulate coral *Syringopora*
Silurian – Carboniferous

colonial, rugose coral
Lithostrotion Carboniferous

small, solitary, scleractine coral
Parasmilia Cretaceous – Recent

Lower Ordovician to Jurassic but they are only important in the Palaeozoic. In members of this group the septae are small or absent while the tabulae are well developed. All tabulate corals are colonial but the corallites are less closely joined than in colonial members of the other two groups. In cross-section they may have a chain-like appearance while in vertical section the long corallites may resemble a series of parallel tubes or a tangle of roots.

Rugose and scleractine corals

The most important Palaeozoic corals are members of the order Rugosa and range from the Ordovician to Permian being particularly important in Silurian, Devonian and Carboniferous rocks. Rugose corals may be solitary or colonial and septae are important in the corallites while tabulae and dissepiments may also be present. Rugose corals were replaced at the beginning of the Mesozoic by members of the order Scleractinia. These corals are very similar in structure to the rugose corals. In them the septae are important and are usually arranged in a plan based on multiples of six. Scleractine corals may be solitary or colonial and they first occur in the Middle Triassic of Europe. The most important members of the group are the reef-building corals. Reefs first occur in the Upper Triassic and this has been an important rock-forming function of corals since Triassic times.

Bryozoa

In Britain this group is also known as the Polyzoa. Bryozoans, or moss animals as they are popularly known, are often found as encrustations on fossil shells, sea urchin plates or rocks. They are colonial and aquatic, the great majority living in the sea and only a few inhabiting freshwater. They are important as fossils in rocks of Ordovician to Recent age. Specimens may be collected from weathered surfaces but better material can be obtained by treating limestones with a weak (three per cent) solution of hydrochloric acid. This dissolves the rock and causes the bryozoans to project slightly from the surface. Specimens may also be washed out of clays. Many bryozoans form encrustations but others may form nodules and some have fern-like growth forms. These are rarely found as complete specimens and 'frond' fragments are more usually discovered.

The classification of bryozoans is based upon fine structure and identification is very difficult, usually requiring study of the microscopic anatomy in thin or polished sections.

net-like bryozoan
Fenestella Ordovician – Permian

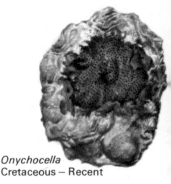

Onychocella
Cretaceous – Recent

Archimedes Carboniferous – Permian
axis carries net-like fronds

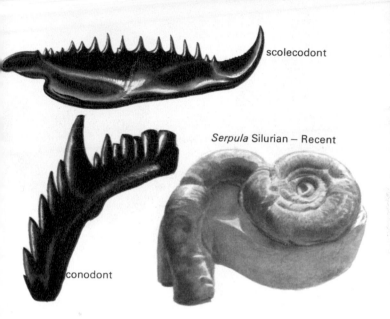

scolecodont

Serpula Silurian – Recent

conodont

Annelids

The familiar worms such as the earthworm, lugworm and ragworm
are grouped in the phylum Annelida. Most members of this group
lack hard parts and are therefore poorly represented in the fossil
record. However, their tracks, burrows and casts are encountered
fairly frequently as fossils and some forms such as *Serpula* secrete
calcareous living tubes that are often found preserved on shells or
rocks. The soft parts of worms are also sometimes preserved in
sedimentary rocks that have very fine textures. Tracks and burrows
of worms are known from the Precambrian and annelids have a
patchy fossil record in rocks of middle Cambrian to Recent age.
The annelid body is soft but many marine worms have horny jaws
composed of chitin or silica. These are minute but occur as fossils
and are known as scolecodonts. They are common in Middle
Palaeozoic rocks but require specialist knowledge for their study.

Conodonts

These are tiny, tooth-like fossils similar in appearance to scolecodonts but composed of calcium phosphate. They occur in rocks of
Ordovician to Triassic age and are very important for stratigraphic
work in the Palaeozoic.

Dendrograptus
Cambrian –
Carboniferous

Diplograptus
Ordovician – Silurian

Monograptus Silurian

Graptolites

The graptolites (class Graptolithina) form an extinct group that may be related to the ancestral chordates (protochordates). They are colonial, marine and usually planktonic animals that are especially important for dating Ordovician and Silurian rocks. Graptolites have very wide distributions and they evolved quite rapidly. Each graptolite colony consists of a number of branches or stipes which have one or both edges serrated. These serrations represent small cups or thecae (sing. theca) which housed the individuals of the colony.

In life the planktonic graptolites were attached to floating objects by a thread or **nema** at the middle of the colony. Some graptolites hung downwards from the nema and are referred to as **pendent** while others grew upwards and are referred to as **scandent**. Early grapto-lites such as *Dictyonema* were net-like but in Ordovician times these were largely replaced by branched forms.

In the field, graptolites usually have the appearance of fine mark-ings along the bedding planes of shale. They are usually carbonized (p.8) and are therefore black. To see them it may be necessary to tilt the rock at an angle to the light so that their shiny surfaces contrast with the duller rock surface.

Molluscs

Snails, squids, cockles and mussels are familiar living members of the Mollusca which is the most important phylum of fossil animals. All molluscs are soft-bodied but they usually have a hard outer shell composed of calcium carbonate. The lower part of the body is usually modified as a fleshy foot which the animal uses in locomotion. Many forms are, however, fixed or sessile as adults while some have developed specialized methods of swimming.

Gastropods

Members of this class are often referred to as snails and all important fossil forms have shells that are usually coiled and enclose the soft parts. Several technical terms are used in the description of the gastropod shell. A complete turn of the shell is a **whorl** and the last whorl ends in an **aperture** through which the foot protrudes. The line along which successive whorls join is called a **suture** and a strong swelling of the shell near the suture is called a **shoulder**. If the shell is flattened between the shoulder and suture this region is called a **ramp**. The lower (front) end of the aperture may be produced as a **canal**. The **columella** is the central column of the shell about which coiling occurs; if this region is hollow it is called an **umbilicus**. Any grooves, tubercles or swellings of the surface are called **sculpturing**. Usually only the shell is preserved and its shape, coiling,

Terminology diagram of a gastropod shell.

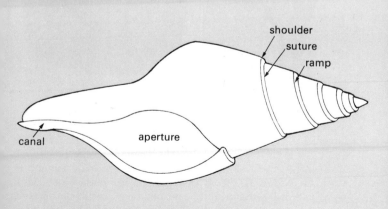

sculpturing and details of the aperture are important for identification.

Gastropods are known from the Lower Cambrian but they only become important in the Ordovician while freshwater and terrestrial forms first occur in the Upper Carboniferous. There are over 35 000 living species of gastropods and over 15 000 fossil species are known.

Coiling Uncoiled shells are usually conical with one of the faces sloping more steeply than the other. The best-known, uncoiled gastropods are the limpets which may be found firmly attached to

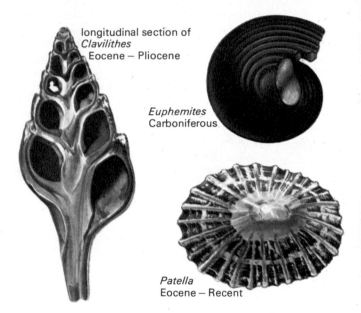

longitudinal section of
Clavilithes
Eocene – Pliocene

Euphemites
Carboniferous

Patella
Eocene – Recent

rocks on the seashore. If the outer whorls of a coiled gastropod surround or cover the inner whorls so that the mid-lines of all the whorls are in the same plane then the coiling is termed **planispiral**. Much the commonest type of coiling is the **conispiral** method in which the whorls rise from the aperture (see illustration). Most gastropods coil so that with the apex pointing upwards the aperture is on the right as you look at it. This is called **dextral** coiling. If the aperture is on the left it is termed **sinistral** coiling.

Palaeozoic gastropods Palaeozoic gastropods belong to two main groups, the Amphigastropoda and the Prosobranchia. Members of the first class usually have symmetrical shells that are either uncoiled or show planispiral coiling. Amphigastropods range from the Cambrian to Triassic and they are relatively rare as fossils. The planispirally coiled *Bellerophon* and *Euphemites* are well-known members of this group.

The class Prosobranchia includes most of the Palaeozoic gastropods and prosobranchs are also important in the Mesozoic and Caenozoic. They have conical or conispiral shells and many

Bellerophon
Silurian – Triassic

Poleumita
Silurian

Platyceras
Silurian – Permian

Palaeozoic members of the group are characterized by the presence of a deep notch or slit on the outer lip of the aperture. During growth the existence of this slit causes a ridge or kink to be developed in the sculpturing of the whorl face. This is known as a **selenizone** and is clearly shown on the face of *Poleumita*. The genus *Platyceras* is a prosobranch having a very large last whorl and a reduced asymmetrical upper region: it usually lacks sculpturing having a smooth shell as in most Palaeozoic gastropods.

Planorbis
Oligocene – Recent

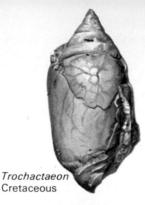

Trochactaeon
Cretaceous

Mesozoic gastropods During Mesozoic times sculpturing of the shell became increasingly important and a host of pronounced and complex patterns developed. Also the lips of the aperture developed complications in many species. These may take the form of a series of strong ridges on the inner lip as in *Trochactaeon*. Strong anterior canals are found in many species and in some Mesozoic genera the outer lip becomes expanded as a large flare.

Caenozoic gastropods Gastropods were important in Mesozoic rocks but it is in Caenozoic deposits that they reach their greatest diversity and abundance. They are particularly abundant in the Eocene and Oligocene of Europe, and Upper Eocene deposits in the Barton region of southern Hampshire, England, have yielded large collections of diverse and beautiful fossil shells. *Clavilithes* is a large gastropod with a well-developed canal and a large last whorl. The spire is steep and the whorls are clearly defined with a strong ramp between the shoulder and the suture. *Ficus* is a much smaller gastropod with a net-like pattern. The last whorl is strong and earlier whorls are small. *Ficus* survives in tropical seas and its presence in the Barton fauna indicates the existence of warm-water conditions in Eocene times. *Hippochrenes* has a very large last whorl and a well-developed canal. Its most characteristic feature is the greatly expanded outer lip of the aperture which forms a huge shelly plate with its inner edge fused to the spire. In contrast to these genera, *Xenophora* has a low shell with a medium-sized last whorl and a wide umbilicus. The Barton species (*Xenophora agglutinans*) is characterized by a strange feature of the shell which often has small particles of foreign matter such as small stones or pieces of shell cemented to its surface.

The Pliocene and Pleistocene rocks of Europe are also rich in fossil gastropods. These may usually be identified to the generic level by reference to living forms with whelks (*Buccinum*), winkles (*Littorina*) and many other familiar forms represented.

Freshwater and land-living gastropods originated in Carboniferous times but it is only in the Caenozoic that their remains become common and they may be used as indicators of environments and for dating Tertiary and Pleistocene sediments. This group includes familiar freshwater snails such as *Viviparus*, *Planorbis* and *Lymnaea* which are known from the European Pleistocene as well as land snails such as *Helix* and *Cepea*.

Marginella
Eocene – Recent

Xenophora
Cretaceous – Recent

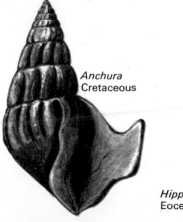

Anchura
Cretaceous

Hippochrenes
Eocene

Cephalopods

Living members of the class Cephalopoda include the octopus, squid, cuttlefish, and the nautilus which occurs in the Pacific and is often encountered as an ornamental shell. Two extinct groups – the ammonites and belemnites – are of great importance as fossils.

Ammonites Ammonites originated in Devonian times and survived until the end of the Cretaceous. They were particularly diverse and abundant during Mesozoic times and are widely used for stratigraphic work on Mesozoic rocks as they evolved very rapidly and many were widely dispersed.

Most ammonites have planispiral shells consisting of a series of chambers that increase in size outwards. These chambers are separated from each other by thin cross-walls or **septae** (sing. septum) and a narrow tube – the **siphuncle** – runs through each chamber near its outer edge. The siphuncle shows as a small circle in cross-section. The line along which the whorls meet is called a **seam** and the **umbilicus** is the depression on each side of the ammonite. The **umbilical shoulder** is the region where the shell turns inwards from the side face towards the seam. A ridge or **keel** may be present along the outer surface and the centre of the outer face is called the **venter**. The region where the septum meets the wall of the ammonite is called a **suture**. It is usually clearly visible on internal moulds, but

Terminology diagram of an ammonite shell.

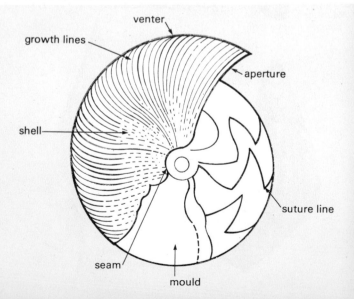

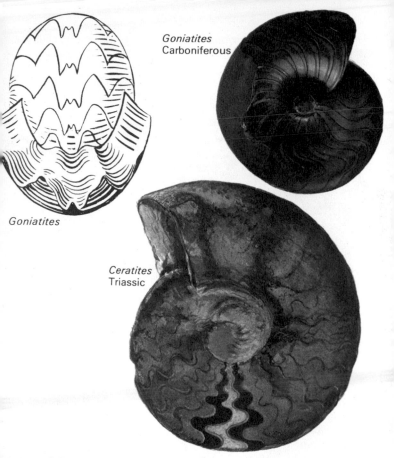

Goniatites

Goniatites
Carboniferous

Goniatites

Ceratites
Triassic

Top left The septum runs across the shell joining the shell wall at the suture line. Specimens sometimes break along the suture line.
Above Wavy suture line is shown at the junction of the colours.

if the actual shell of the ammonite is preserved then it may carry numerous growth lines and will obscure the suture. In this case it is necessary to remove part of the shell, to expose the inner surface, before the suture can be studied. The pattern of the suture is very important for identification of ammonites. Suture diagrams are usually shown with illustrations of ammonites and they are made by drawing the suture as if the shell had been flattened out from seam to seam with the venter at the middle. In the diagram the

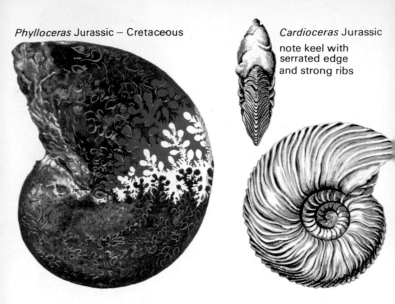

Phylloceras Jurassic – Cretaceous

Cardioceras Jurassic

note keel with serrated edge and strong ribs

venter carries an arrow that points towards the aperture. Different parts of the suture have different names. A **lobe** is any backward swelling of the suture and in the suture diagram this would be shown as a downward inflexion of the line while a **saddle** is a forward swelling of the suture and therefore projects upwards on the suture diagram. Thus lobes and saddles appear to alternate from left to right. Complications of the suture occur, as sub-divisions of the lobes and saddles are produced, and these are very important for identification.

Ammonites from the Devonian all have simple sutures similar to those of *Goniatites*, in which the lobes and saddles are undivided. Forms with this 'goniatitic suture' are also the most common ammonites in Carboniferous rocks and they persist into the Triassic, though they are very rare above the Permian. In the Carboniferous, forms with more complex sutures appear. These ammonites have a suture pattern that has rounded saddles and serrated lobes, and this pattern is called 'ceratitic' after the genus *Ceratites*, in which it is well developed. In Permian times ammonites with goniatitic and ceratitic sutures were common, but a new and more complex suture pattern also appeared. This is known as the 'ammonite suture' and is very complex with divided lobes and saddles. This type of suture is well developed in *Phylloceras*. In the Triassic, ammonites with the ammonitic suture pattern are less common than those with ceratitic sutures. Also during the Triassic, ornamentation of ribs, keels and ridges begins to be an important feature of ammonites. Only forms with the ammonitic suture pattern are known from Jurassic rocks and strong ornamentation is common. In the Cretaceous, ammonitic sutures are still dominant, but towards the end of Cretaceous times some forms evolved simpler sutures which resemble the ceratitic type. In Jurassic and Cretaceous times the ammonites were at the peak of their development and a variety of coiling forms occurred, with loosely coiled, straight, 'U'-shaped and conispiral forms occurring. The ammonites became extinct at the end of the Mesozoic and their decline and extinction was as important in the marine faunas as was the extinction of the dinosaurs on land.

The Lower Jurassic, European ammonite *Amaltheus* is a flattened form which has a characteristic ornamentation with a very strong keel that carries a series of small notches on either side. It has a well-developed ammonitic suture pattern. *Placenticeras* is common in the Cretaceous and is characterized by the venter which is flattened or carries a central channel. It also has an ammonitic suture pattern. The Cretaceous *Hamites* and *Scaphites* have bizarre coiling forms.

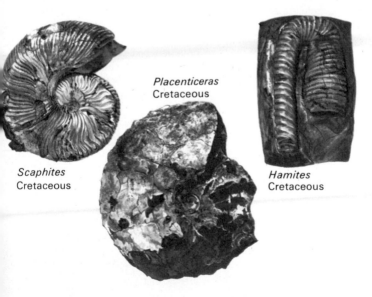

Placenticeras
Cretaceous

Scaphites
Cretaceous

Hamites
Cretaceous

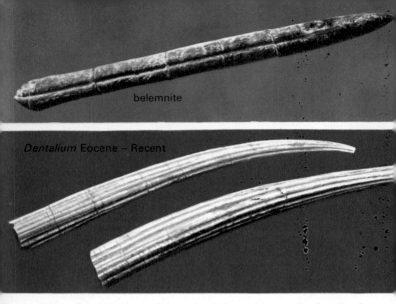

belemnite

Dentalium Eocene – Recent

Belemnites Members of the order Belemnoida are closely related to the living squids and cuttlefish. The fossil belemnite shell represents a completely internal structure similar to the pen of squids or cuttle bone. Belemnites are extinct and are usually found as bullet-shaped fossils. They first appear in rocks of Palaeozoic age but are only common in the Mesozoic, being particularly abundant in the Jurassic and Cretaceous. The bullet-shaped part of the belemnite is called the **rostrum** and in life it was positioned with the point towards the back of the animal. Very well-preserved specimens carry a thin-walled hollow region at the front (blunt) end of the rostrum. This is called the **phragmocone**. It is chambered and in life the front chamber housed some of the soft parts of the animal.

Scaphopods

Members of the small molluscan class Scaphopoda, have long, slender, tubular shells, that are open at both ends and often carry fine growth lines running around the shell and ridges of varying strength running along the shell. Living scaphopods are also known as tusk shells and they live buried, almost upright in soft sand, with the narrow end (back) projecting above the surface of the seabed. Fossil scaphopods range from the Silurian and they are most abundant in the Caenozoic. They may be locally abundant but in general scaphopods are rare as fossils.

Bivalve molluscs

The bivalve molluscs belong to the class Pelecypoda which is also known as the Lamellibranchia or the Bivalvia. They are familiar as the living mussels, clams, cockles, scallops and oysters. Several features of the bivalve shell are important for their study. The height, length, thickness and general shape are often characteristic and many forms have ornamentation. The **beak** is a pointed or rounded region above the **hinge line**, which is the region along which the valves articulate. Several internal features of the valves are also important. The part of the shell immediately below the beak is called the **cardinal** region and parts in front and behind this are termed **lateral**. In many bivalves there are projections of shell along the hinge line. These relate to the opening and closing of the valves and are called **teeth**. A flattened region between the hinge line and the beak is an **area**. Muscle scars are flat, smooth and usually rounded parts of the inner face of each valve. The presence and size of these scars are important and the muscles, which in life attach to these regions, are used for closing the valves. Some bivalves are able to protrude a fleshy tube or **siphon** from the shell and the foot may also be protruded. In parts of the shell where this occurs the margins may be flexed so that a permanent opening or **gape** may be present.

Terminology diagrams of a bivalve shell.

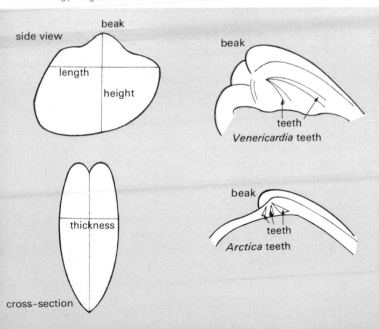

Mytilus
Triassic – Recent

auricles

Ostrea
Triassic –
Recent

Pecten
Eocene – Recent

Gryphaea
Jurassic –
Eocene

Mussels, oysters and scallops These three kinds of bivalve molluscs are characterized by the reduction or absence of hinge teeth. Many mussels (suborder Mytilacea) have shells similar to that of the living mussel, *Mytilus*, in which the beak is shifted to the front of the valve. Very small hinge teeth are sometimes present in members of this group. Mussels range from the Ordovician to Recent and they often form large beds containing thousands or millions of shells.

Oysters (suborder Ostreacea) form one of the most important groups of bivalves. They are known from the Triassic to Recent and are characterized by their extremely thick valves. Usually one valve is larger than the other and the smaller valve is usually also flatter; they are therefore said to be **inequivalve**. In life the larger valve is usually cemented to rocks or other shells. Oysters lack hinge teeth. The living *Ostrea* occurs throughout the Mesozoic and Caenozoic. *Gryphaea* is also a very important fossil oyster.

Scallops are important as fossils. True scallops such as *Pecten* have rounded, almost symmetrical valves, often with wings or auricles near the beak and a coarse ornamentation of ridges is common. Scallops lack teeth and many are inequivalve and have asymmetrical shells.

Ark shells, nut shells and freshwater mussels Many bivalve molluscs having numerous small teeth are grouped in the order Taxodonta, which was important in the Palaeozoic and is still well represented in living marine faunas. Small taxodonts usually have almost symmetrical shells with the beak near the mid-line and many small hinge teeth. The nut shell, *Nucula*, is typical of this group. In contrast the larger forms are often very asymmetrical with one side elongate. In these forms some of the teeth tend to be nearly parallel to the hinge line and a large cardinal area is often present. Living members of this group include the ark shell, *Arca*, while both *Arca* and *Parallelodon* are important fossil forms.

Members of another important bivalve group, the Schizodonta, have a few relatively large hinge teeth concentrated beneath the beak. Typical members of this group are *Trigonia* and *Unio*. *Trigonia* has two, large, divergent teeth that have ridged edges. Its ornamentation is characteristic, with the pattern on the back region very different from that on the rest of the shell. *Trigonia* is represented today by a few species that live in the Pacific, but it is well known as a fossil

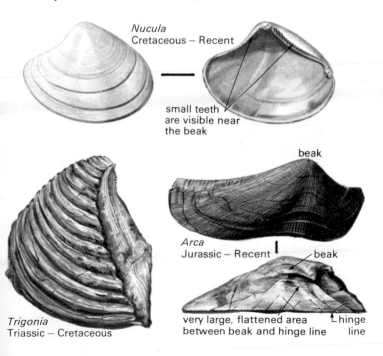

Nucula
Cretaceous – Recent

small teeth
are visible near
the beak

beak

Arca
Jurassic – Recent

beak

Trigonia
Triassic – Cretaceous

very large, flattened area   hinge
between beak and hinge line   line

from Europe. The dentition of the freshwater mussel, *Unio*, consists of a few teeth beneath the beak and thin, elongate teeth almost parallel to the hinge line in the lateral regions. *Unio* ranges from the Triassic to Recent.

Clams and cockles The familiar living clams and cockles represent an important group of bivalve molluscs, in which the hinge teeth are very well developed in the cardinal region. They range from the Silurian to Recent and may now be at the peak of their development. Primitive clams such as *Arctica* have two or three, well-developed hinge teeth in the cardinal region, while more advanced forms such as *Astarte* have well-developed cardinal teeth and a few clearly defined lateral teeth. The most advanced clams and cockles are represented by *Venericardia*, which has two anterior and two posterior lateral teeth on its right valve and three large cardinals on each valve. *Venericardia* is a large, widely distributed, Cretaceous and Caenozoic bivalve, and has a radial ornamentation of flat-topped ribs. The living cockle, *Cerastoderma*, has two large cardinal teeth, well-developed lateral teeth, and an ornamentation of very prominent ribs.

Rudists The rudist molluscs (order Pachyodonta) are the most bizarre of the bivalve molluscs. Rudists are sedentary or fixed as adults, with one valve lying above the other. The lower valve is modified to form a thick-walled, elongate cone, which carries strong longitudinal ribs on its surface in many species. The upper valve is small and flattened forming a lid for the lower valve. It was opened by being moved vertically. Rudists are very similar in appearance to some of the corals. They are confined to rocks of Cretaceous age and appear to have been reef-living forms that were confined to warm-water conditions. *Hippurites* is a relatively small rudist but some species were very large.

Burrowing and boring bivalves Many bivalve molluscs have adopted a burrowing or boring way of life. The cockles and clams mentioned above are mainly burrowers but their shells show little specialization for this way of life, in comparison with the valves of the razor shell, *Ensis*, which has a greatly elongated shell with permanent gapes at either end. More advanced boring forms such as *Teredo* have reduced shells with large permanent gapes. The shells of *Teredo* are rarely discovered as fossils but their borings may be encountered as trace fossils in fossil wood.

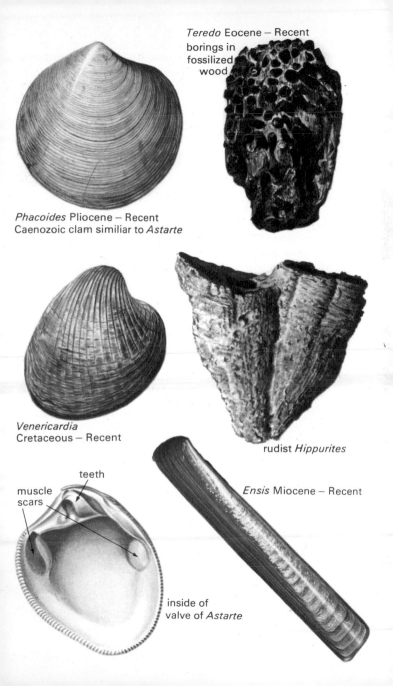

Teredo Eocene – Recent borings in fossilized wood

Phacoides Pliocene – Recent
Caenozoic clam similiar to *Astarte*

Venericardia
Cretaceous – Recent

rudist *Hippurites*

Ensis Miocene – Recent

teeth

muscle scars

inside of valve of *Astarte*

Brachiopods

Members of the phylum Brachiopoda are a relatively minor element of living marine faunas where they are represented by about 250 species. They were, however, very important as fossils and over 30 000 fossil species are recognized. Brachiopods have bivalve shells and may therefore be confused with bivalve molluscs. However, a number of simple differences allow members of the two groups to be distinguished. In bivalve molluscs each valve is usually asymmetrical – that is to say, the front and back parts are not mirror images – and the beak usually points towards the front. The two valves of the bivalve mollusc are usually similar and are mirror images of each other – oysters and many scallops are exceptions to this. In contrast, each brachiopod valve is usually symmetrical with the beak lying in the mid-line, and one valve is always larger than the other. Some of the terms used to describe brachiopods are the same as those used for bivalve molluscs. In brachiopods the animal usually rests on one of its valves and this lower valve carries a

Terminology diagrams of a brachiopod shell.

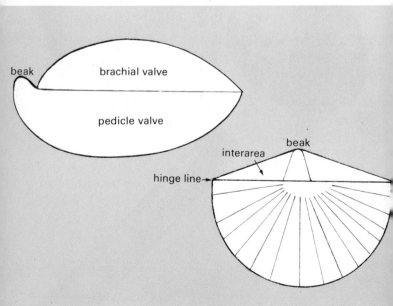

Lingula Ordovician – Recent

Crania Cretaceous – Recent

specimens
are attached
to a strophomenid

muscular attachment organ known as the **pedicle**. The lower valve
is therefore termed the **pedicle valve** and always has the stronger
beak. The upper valve carries an organ known as the **lophophore**,
which may consist of a disc or of long branches (brachia) that form
folds or spirals. Hair-like processes on the lophophore produce a
current of water, from which the food particles are extracted. The
lophophore is rarely visible in fossils but its form is very important
in the classification of brachiopods and is studied either in specially
treated fossils or by making a series of sections of the fossil. The
upper valve is called the **brachial valve**. As in the bivalve molluscs
the **hinge line** is the region along which the valves articulate. The
interarea is a flattened region between the hinge line and the beak.
Sometimes the beak of the pedicle valve carries a small hole, the
foramen, through which the pedicle emerges during life.

Brachiopods range from the Lower Cambrian to Recent. Two
major groups, the Inarticulata and Articulata, are recognized. The
latter have hinged valves while the valves of the inarticulate brachiopods are held together by muscles.

Inarticulate brachiopods

The inarticulate brachiopods range from the Lower Cambrian to
Recent, but they have never been common. The inarticulate shell

Spirifer
Carboniferous

Orthis
Cambrian — Ordovician

Leptaena
Ordovician — Devonian

Platystrophia
Ordovician — Silurian

is usually very thin and is composed mainly of calcium phosphate, whereas the shells of articulate brachiopods are calcareous. The living genus *Lingula* is one of the largest members of the group, with a shell ranging up to five centimetres long. *Lingula* is elongate and almost like a fingernail in appearance. It is one of the oldest known genera of animals and ranges as far back as the Ordovician.

Articulate brachiopods

These are brachiopods with calcareous shells in which the valves are hinged. The spirifers (order Spiriferida) are a very common and diverse, extinct group of brachiopods. In spirifers the lophophore carries spiral brachia, which may sometimes be visible on broken or weathered specimens, but it is often very difficult to assign spirifers to their group on the basis of external features. Spirifers range from the Ordovician to Jurassic and they are particularly important in Devonian and Carboniferous rocks.

In contrast to the spirifers the orthids (order Orthida) can usually be assigned to their group on the basis of external features. Orthids usually have biconvex shells with long hinge lines and interareas on both valves. Their outlines range from almost circular to almost elliptical and an ornamentation of radiating ribs is often present.

Orthids range through rocks of Lower Cambrian to Permian age but they are especially important in the Ordovician.

Orthis is a typical orthid brachiopod. It has a long hinge line that is also the widest part of the shell. There are clearly defined interareas on both valves and beneath the beak a small triangular swelling may be present on each interarea. The orthid *Schizophoria* is strongly biconvex with a shorter hinge line and small interareas. It has a pattern of fine, radiating ridges and a deep, wide groove on the pedicle valve.

Strophomenid brachiopods (order Strophomenida) may have interareas on one or both valves but in contrast to the orthids one valve is usually convex and the other concave. Either valve may be convex and you should look at the beak to get the correct orientation before attempting identification. For example, *Strophomena* has a convex brachial valve and concave pedicle valve while *Chonetes* has a concave brachial valve and convex pedicle valve. Strophomenids usually have lone hinge lines and an ornamentation of fine ridges. They range from the Ordovician to Recent and are especially common in Middle Ordovician to Upper Permian rocks.

The Pentamerids (order Pentamerida) have short hinge lines and biconvex shells. They are less important than the preceding group, ranging only from the Cambrian to the Devonian and being important only in the Silurian and Lower Devonian.

Strophomena Ordovician

Chonetes Devonian

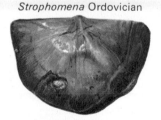

Schizophoria Devonian − Permian

Conchidium Silurian − Devonian

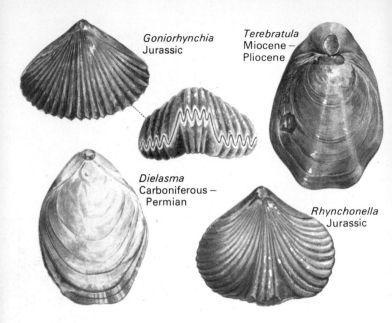

Goniorhynchia
Jurassic

Terebratula
Miocene –
Pliocene

Dielasma
Carboniferous –
Permian

Rhynchonella
Jurassic

Mesozoic and Caenozoic brachiopods

The two most important Mesozoic and Caenozoic brachiopod groups are the terebratulids (order Terebratulida) and the rhynchonellids (order Rhynchonellida) but the spirifers are still fairly well represented in the Lower Mesozoic and the strophomenids and inarticulate brachiopods still survive. Terebratulids usually have almost circular or elongate shells with very short hinge lines. A small interarea occurs on the pedicle valve and ornamentation is rarely stronger than fine ridges. A foramen is present. Terebratulids have been common since Triassic times and they comprise over half the living brachiopods. *Dielasma* and *Terebratula* are typical members of this group. They both have strongly biconvex shells that lack any marked ornamentation, but each has a clearly visible foramen.

Rhynchonellids are usually relatively small, biconvex brachiopods with strongly ridged shells. Their outlines range from almost triangular to rounded. The hinge line is short and interareas are not usually visible, though they may be present on one or both valves. Rhynchonellids range from the Ordovician to Recent and they are most common in Jurassic and Cretaceous rocks.

Arthropods

The Arthropoda is the largest phylum of animals and contains more genera and species than all other animal groups combined. In the sea and freshwater the group is represented by the crustaceans – crabs, lobsters, shrimps, etc. – the king crabs, some insects and the sea spiders, while the trilobites are among the most numerous of all fossils in Palaeozoic rocks. Arthropods are the only invertebrates that have been really successful on land, where the group is represented by the spiders, scorpions, centipedes, millipedes, and crustaceans; while there are a host of terrestrial insects many of which are capable of active flight.

Most arthropods have segmented bodies that are covered with a hard cuticle composed of chitin. In crustaceans and some other arthropods the cuticle is further hardened by impregnation with calcium carbonate and calcium phosphate. The presence of a hard cuticle means that growth must occur in stages with periodic moulting of the cuticle to allow increase in size, and many fossil trilobites represent only the shed cuticle coating.

In primitive arthropods every segment of the body carries a pair of limbs, but in the majority of advanced members of the group the walking limbs are concentrated in one part of the body while in other parts the limbs are lost or have evolved into feeding structures

Recent arthropods

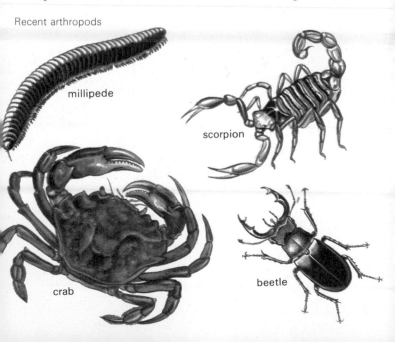

millipede

scorpion

crab

beetle

or sense organs. The limbs are also enclosed in chitin and are jointed. In many aquatic arthropods parts of the limbs are modified as respiratory organs.

Trilobites

The class Trilobita contains the most important large fossil arthropods. They are restricted to the Palaeozoic and are especially abundant in Cambrian and Ordovician rocks. The trilobite body is divided into a head or **cephalon**, a **thorax** and a tail or **pygidium**. It is also divided along its length into a central **axis** with **pleural regions** at each side. Some of the technical terms applied to trilobites are shown in the figure. Important features for identifying trilobites are: details of the head, particularly the genal angle or presence of a genal spine; the eyes and details of the front border and glabella; on the thorax, details of the pleural lobes and the number of segments; on the pygidium, details of the back border and the number of segments.

Trilobites were entirely marine and most of them crawled or burrowed in the seabed. They had jointed limbs and antennae but these are rarely preserved. Trilobites first occur in the Lower Cambrian, but in these rocks they are a diverse group, which suggests that they originated in Precambrian times. Four orders of

Terminology diagram of a trilobite.

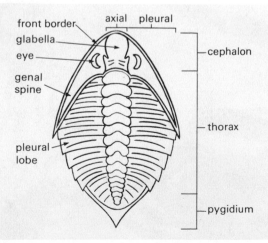

Olenellus Cambrian

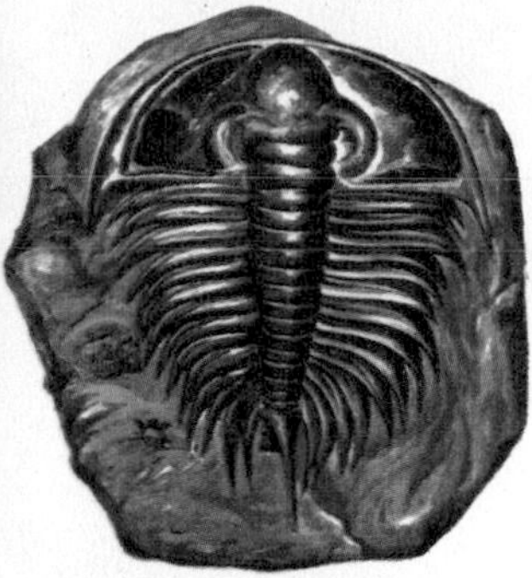

Paedeumias Cambrian protoparian trilobite

Paradoxides Cambrian

Bumastus Ordovician – Silurian

trilobites are known from the Cambrian and members of these groups exhibit several distinctive features.

Protoparian trilobites (order Protoparia) are the oldest members of the group and are restricted to the Lower Cambrian. *Olenellus* is a typical protoparian. It has large eyes, genal spines and a glabella carrying three or four furrows. The front border is clearly defined, the thorax consists of many segments and the pygidium is small.

The opisthoparian trilobites (order Opisthoparia) occur a little later than the first protoparians and range from the Lower Cambrian to the Permian. This is the largest order of trilobites and the Middle Cambrian genus *Paradoxides* is typical of this group. It has a facial suture that runs across the facial region from front to back,

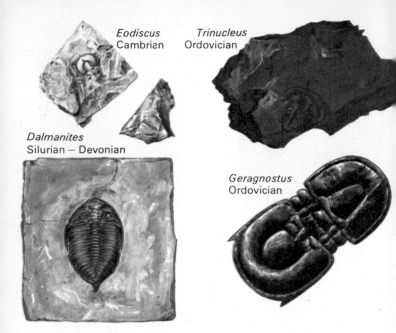

Eodiscus
Cambrian

Trinucleus
Ordovician

Dalmanites
Silurian – Devonian

Geragnostus
Ordovician

skirting the inner edge of the crescentic eye. The thorax consists of many segments and the pygidium is again small. *Paradoxides* is a large trilobite and some opisthoparians reach almost a metre in length. *Bumastus* is an opisthoparian in which all trace of the axis and segmentation of the head have been lost.

Members of the order Eodiscida are known from the Lower and Middle Cambrian. This group includes small to minute trilobites such as *Eodiscus* in which the head and pygidium are almost equal in size. *Eodiscus* has no eyes, its thorax consists of three segments and the pygidium has a segmented axis.

Another order of small trilobites is the Agnostida (Cambrian–Ordovician) and members of this group are superficially similar to *Eodiscus. Geragnostus* is typical of the group. It has large head and tail regions and there are only two thoracic segments. *Geragnostus* has no eyes and there is no segmentation of the pygidium axis.

At the end of early Cambrian times the protoparians became extinct but in middle Cambrian times a new trilobite order, the Proparia, arose. This order includes some of the best known trilobites with *Dalmanites, Calymene* and *Phacops* as typical proparians.

All have well-developed eyes and the facial suture is developed on the upper surface of the head. They may be distinguished by features of the head, in particular the eyes and glabella, and by details of the pygidium. *Dalmanites* and *Calymene* both occur in the Silurian rocks of Dudley, Worcestershire which is a famous area for collecting trilobites.

A further new order, the Hypoparia, first occurs in the Lower Ordovician. *Trinucleus* is typical of this group. Its most striking feature is the wide flattened band around the head and the long genal spines.

Insects

The majority of living arthropods are members of the subphylum Insecta (insects) which includes over 700 000 described species. Most insects have wings and three pairs of jointed legs on the middle part of the body or thorax. Insects are mainly terrestrial and they are relatively rare as fossils when compared with their abundance in living faunas. They range from the Devonian to Recent and are now at the peak of their development. Some of the most popularly known fossil insects are those preserved in amber, which is itself fossil resin. An insect in amber consists of the complete body of the animal with even its colour preserved. You will not be able to collect insects in amber but they are sometimes seen as jewellery or on sale

insect in amber

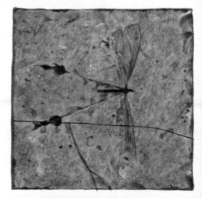

insect on a block
from the Oligocene
of Europe

as curios. Miocene rocks at Oeningen in Germany have yielded the remains of numerous insects that are beautifully preserved in the fine grained rock, which also contain the remains of numerous plants on which the insects presumably lived.

Giant water scorpions

The eurypterids (class Merostomata) are also known as giant water scorpions but in fact they are more closely related to the living king crabs. This group includes the largest known fossil arthropods with some almost three metres in length. *Pterygotus* occurs in the Upper Silurian of Scotland and is one of the largest eurypterids with big chelicerae or pincers, large eyes and a flattened tail. Many other eurypterids had smaller chelicerae and eyes, and pointed tails. The habitat of the eurypterids is not definitely known but it is thought that they lived in estuaries and lagoons where they preyed on smaller invertebrates and possibly early fishes.

Crabs, lobsters and barnacles

These are members of the subphylum Crustacea which is the most important group of marine and freshwater arthropods and includes over 26 000 living species. Crustaceans usually have a hard outer coating that consists of the same material as the insect coating, chitin, impregnated with calcium carbonate, and this hard 'exo-

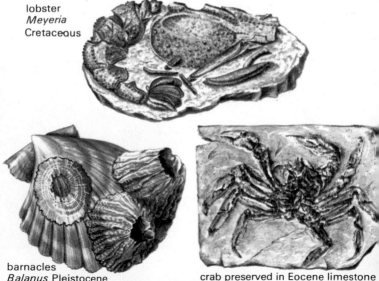

lobster
Meyeria
Cretaceous

barnacles
Balanus Pleistocene

crab preserved in Eocene limestone

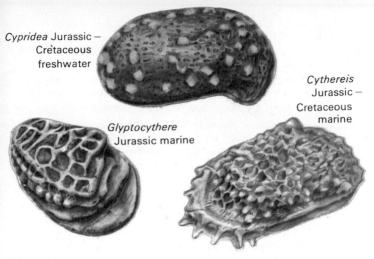

Cypridea Jurassic – Cretaceous freshwater

Cythereis Jurassic – Cretaceous marine

Glyptocythere Jurassic marine

Ostracods

skeleton' is frequently fossilized. Crustaceans have many more walking legs than insects, and their bodies are not clearly divided into a head, thorax and abdomen. Crustaceans first occur in the Cambrian but with the exception of the ostracods their remains are relatively rare in rocks lower than Middle Mesozoic.

Ostracods Ostracods (subphylum Crustacea, class Ostracoda) are tiny marine and freshwater crustaceans that have shells similar to those of minute bivalve molluscs. The hinge is carried as the upper edge of the shell and the legs are fully enclosed by the two valves which are opened for feeding and swimming. Ostracods range from the Ordovician to Recent and their small size, abundance, wide dispersal and rapid change of species make them the most important of the arthropods in stratigraphical work and as they are also common in freshwater deposits, where forams are absent, they have very great stratigraphic importance. Ostracods range in size from less than half a millimetre to a maximum of two centimetres but the majority of them are less than five millimetres long and they must therefore be collected by special techniques and studied under a microscope. Fossil ostracods are grouped according to the external features of their shells which are usually almost oval but vary in size, convexity and features of the hinge and carry a variety of patterns consisting of ridges, lumps, pores, spines, depressions and pits.

Echinoderms

Starfishes and sea urchins are among the most familiar marine invertebrates. They represent the phylum Echinodermata which originated in Precambrian times and has a fossil record beginning in the Lower Cambrian. There are over 5 000 known species of echinoderms and the phylum is divided into two groups with one including those echinoderms such as the starfishes and sea urchins that are free-living as adults, while the other includes forms such as the sea lilies and cystoids that are usually attached during their adult life.

Echinoderms are exclusively marine and their main characteristic is the body arrangement which is based on a radial symmetry with five parts arranged around a central point. This is termed **pentaradial symmetry**. The echinoderm body contains a system of canals that are similar in function to the circulatory system of other animals. In echinoderms, however, this system circulates seawater rather than blood and is termed the 'water vascular system'.

The fixed echinoderms (subphylum Pelmatozoa) are included in several classes of which the sea lilies and blastoids are mentioned later. Other important pelmatozoans are the edrioasteroids and cystoids.

Edrioasteroids (class Edrioasteroidea) range from the Lower

Cystoids

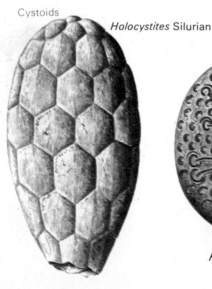

Holocystites Silurian

Proteocystites Devonian

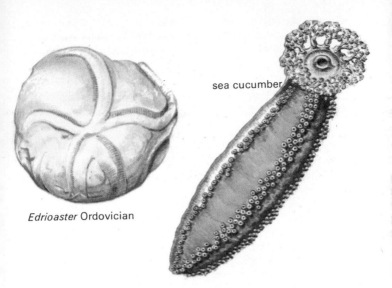

sea cucumber

Edrioaster Ordovician

Cambrian to the Carboniferous. They are generally rare but are well known from several areas of North America. The body is disc-like and consists of many small plates. On its upper surface there is a star-shape with the mouth at the centre.

Cystoids (class Cystoidea) range from the Ordovician to Devonian and have almost spherical to sac-like bodies composed of many small plates and carrying arms consisting of double rows of plates that were used in feeding.

The group of free-living echinoderms (subphylum Eleutherozoa) includes the starfishes, sea urchins and the sea cucumbers. Sea cucumbers (class Holothuroidea) are the most atypical of the echinoderms. They have long, bilaterally symmetrical bodies that consist almost entirely of soft tissues but include small spicules composed of silica. Holothuroids are very rare as fossils but the spicules are distributed widely in rocks of Carboniferous and later age. They are extremely small, however, and you are very unlikely to find them.

Sea urchins

A typical sea urchin (class Echinoidea) has a rounded, heart-shaped or disc-shaped body that is coated with a hard test consisting of many fused, rigid plates. The symmetry of the body is based on a five-rayed plan with the mouth on the lower surface and the anus on the upper or the back surface. Living and well-preserved fossil echinoids are covered with spines that are protective and also function in 'walking'. There are two main groups of sea urchins – the regular and irregular echinoids. Sea urchins have been important since Jurassic times, though primitive members of the group are known from rocks of Ordovician and later age.

Regular echinoids Members of the subclass Regularia usually have almost circular tests with the mouth at the centre of the lower surface and the anus immediately above it on the upper surface. The earliest echinoids belong to this group and *Hemicidaris* from the British Jurassic is a typical regular echinoid. The surface of *Hemicidaris* is covered with numerous swellings or tubercles. The largest of these are known as 'primary tubercles' and in life they carried spines which could be moved by means of muscles attached near their bases. The anus of *Hemicidaris* is surrounded by a series of large plates and five, narrow rays with regularly arranged, small tubercles which radiate from the outer edge of this ring of plates. These regions are known as 'ambulacral areas' and in life they carry organs known as 'tube feet' which are used in locomotion and respiration.

Irregular echinoids Members of the subclass Irregularia differ from the above group in having the anus positioned between the back two rays of the test. Most irregular echinoids are oval rather than circular and there is a tendency for members of the group to show bilateral symmetry.

Irregular echinoids are much more common than regular echinoids as fossils and are frequently encountered in the chalk of southern Britain where the two genera *Micraster* and *Conulus* are particularly abundant. *Micraster* is heart-shaped and is known as the 'heart urchin'. It is closely related to the living sea potato, *Spatangus,* which lives buried in sand on the seashore. The mouth of *Micraster* is situated near the front of the lower surface, while the anus is on the side face at the point or back of the heart-shape. The upper surface carries five, radiating, ambulacral areas (rays), four of which are indented and petal-like. *Conulus* has a high, almost circular test with the mouth at the centre of the lower surface giving it the appearance of a regular echinoid. The anus is, however, at the back of the lower surface, clearly indicating that *Conulus* must be grouped with the irregular echinoids.

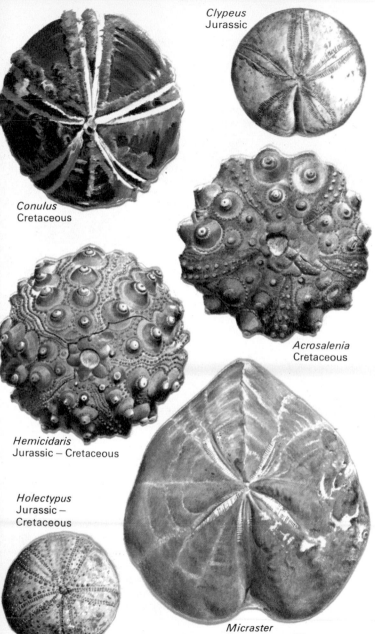

Clypeus
Jurassic

Conulus
Cretaceous

Acrosalenia
Cretaceous

Hemicidaris
Jurassic – Cretaceous

Holectypus
Jurassic –
Cretaceous

Micraster
Cretaceous – Miocene

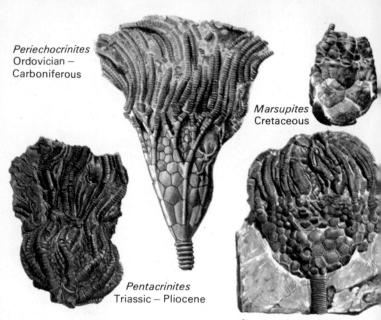

Periechocrinites
Ordovician –
Carboniferous

Marsupites
Cretaceous

Pentacrinites
Triassic – Pliocene

Sagenocrinites Silurian

Sea lilies

Sea lilies (class Crinoidea) are a widely distributed group of living
marine animals. Although they range into deep waters they occur
most frequently in shallow seas and their discovery as fossils may be
interpreted to indicate shallow-water conditions at the time of
deposition. Crinoids are very plant-like in appearance with a
stem that is attached by root-like processes at its base and which
carries the body at its upper end. The stem consists of a column of
plates which have a radial structure and a central opening in cross-
section. The shape of the stem plates may be useful in identification.
For example, the stem plates of *Pentacrinites* are characteristic as
they have a pentagonal to star-shaped cross-section. The importance
of stem plates is increased by the fact that they are the part most
commonly preserved.

The body or theca of the crinoid consists of plates that are large
and usually clearly visible in fossils. Basically the theca consists of
two rows of plates – the **basals** and **radials** – with the basals attaching

to the stem and the radials supporting the arms. Further complications of the theca arise by the addition of extra plates known as **inter-radials** between or above the radials, and by the addition of further plates between and above the inter-radials. The arms are the free, feathery, mobile processes attached to the theca. Basically five arms are present but these may be branched or forked so that effectively there are many more. The arms may also carry numerous feathery processes known as **pinnules**.

There are three main groups of Palaeozoic crinoids – the Inadunata, Flexibalia and Camerata – and the characteristics of these groups are well demonstrated by the genera *Gissocrinus*, *Sagenocrinites* and *Periechocrinites* respectively. In the inadunates the theca consists of a few plates that are firmly joined and the arms are free from their bases. The flexible crinoids have a theca consisting of numerous plates that are not firmly joined. *Sagenocrinites* has many inter-radial plates and short arms. The camerates have their thecal plates firmly joined and the theca consists of numerous plates.

The Mesozoic and Caenozoic crinoids all belong to the subclass Articulata in which the plates of the theca above the radials are usually reduced with often only the radials and basals retained. *Pentacrinites* is a typical member of this group while *Marsupites* is a stemless form that has a large theca consisting of a few large plates.

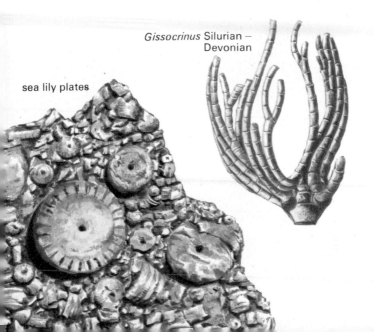

Gissocrinus Silurian – Devonian

sea lily plates

Blastoids

Blastoids (class Blastoidea) are bud-like echinoderms that are known only from the Palaeozoic and may be locally common. The top of the blastoid carries several pores including the mouth and anus, while five, ambulacral grooves radiate downwards from the top. The upper part of each groove runs between a pair of deltoid plates while the lower part is in the notch of a 'V'- or 'U'-shaped radial plate. There are thus five deltoid and five radial plates. At their lower ends the radial plates meet three basal plates of which two are large while one is only half the size of the others. The basal plates join the stem or column.

Starfishes

Starfishes (class Stelleroidea) have less rigid bodies than most other echinoderms and they usually lack large or fused plates. They may be locally abundant as fossils but are in general rare. There are two main subclasses of starfishes. Members of the subclass Asteroidia have thick arms and this group includes the familiar living starfishes, while the more delicate ophiuroids (subclass Ophiuroidia) or brittle stars have long, thin arms that often have a feathery appearance. *Palaeocoma* is a typical Mesozoic ophiuroid while *Pentasteria* is an asteroid with the typical star-shape and *Calliderma* has a very large disc and short arms.

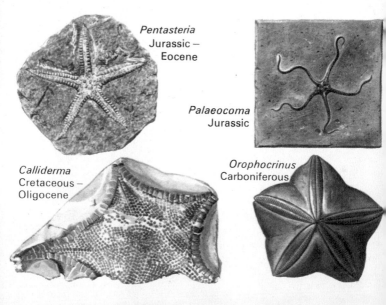

Pentasteria
Jurassic –
Eocene

Palaeocoma
Jurassic

Calliderma
Cretaceous –
Oligocene

Orophocrinus
Carboniferous

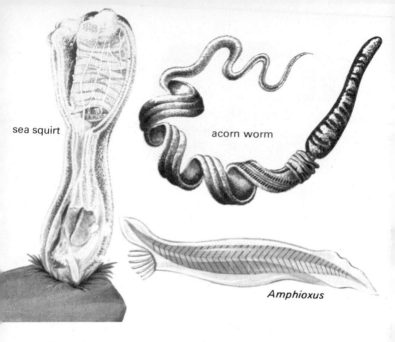

sea squirt

acorn worm

Amphioxus

FOSSIL CHORDATES

The vertebrates are the best known chordates and are the only members of the group that are abundant as fossils. There are, however, several groups of bizarre animals that are either included in the phylum Chordata or in closely related groups. These animals are unimportant as fossils but they give us valuable information about chordate relationships.

Amphioxus is a small fish-like chordate that has a long torpedo-shaped body. There is a row of gill slits near its front end. This is enclosed by a flap of skin and functions in feeding but is very similar to the gill slits of primitive fishes and to the pores of a sea squirt. *Amphioxus* also has a nerve cord running along the upper or dorsal part of its body and below this there is a long stiff rod known as the **notochord**. Gill slits, a dorsal nerve cord and a notochord are always present at some stage in the life history of all chordates. Acorn worms (subphylum Hemichordata) have a small notochord near the front of the body, a small dorsal nerve cord and gill slits. Acorn worms are therefore closely related to the chordates but their larvae are very similar to those of echinoderms which indicates that they are also related to members of this group.

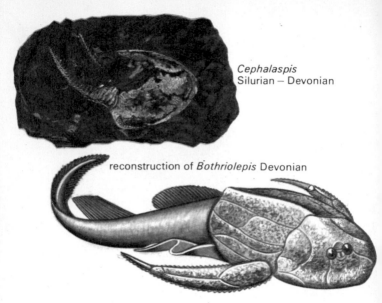

Cephalaspis
Silurian – Devonian

reconstruction of *Bothriolepis* Devonian

Armoured fishes

Vertebrates, or animals with backbones, first occurred in the Ordovician and by Devonian times over ten distinct orders of fishes were established. These primitive fishes are included in two classes, the Agnatha and Placodermi. The name Agnatha means 'without jaws' and the earliest fishes were indeed jawless. The living agnathans – lampreys and hagfish – are quite unlike their Silurian and Devonian relatives for these early fishes were coated with an armour of bony plates. One of the best known fossil agnathans is *Cephalaspis* which occurs in the Upper Silurian and Lower Devonian of Europe and is also recorded from Asia and North America. *Cephalaspis* had a flattened body with the eyes on top of its head. It was probably a freshwater fish that fed by straining food particles from the mud on the beds of streams and rivers.

The placoderms were very heavily armoured fishes that also had internal bony skeletons and jaws. They are mainly restricted to the Devonian and their remains are most frequently discovered as isolated bony plates. *Bothriolepis* is a well-known placoderm that had worldwide distribution in late Devonian times. Its head had a heavy, bony armour consisting of several plates but its tail was naked and carried fins.

Bony fishes

The bony fishes (class Osteichthyes) first occurred in freshwater deposits of Devonian age. By the end of the Palaeozoic they were dominant in all freshwater environments and had also expanded into the seas. Since that time they have expanded steadily, so that they now exceed all other vertebrates combined in numbers of species and genera. If one excludes the sharks and rays then this class includes all other familiar fishes. As the name implies the bony fishes have a skeleton composed of bone, almost all have a complete covering of scales and they usually have a symmetrical tail with the upper and lower parts equal in size. The bones of these fishes are frequently encountered in Mesozoic and Caenozoic deposits but complete fishes are generally rare though they may be very abundant locally. For example, Cretaceous deposits near Beirut, Lebanon have yielded thousands of complete fossil fishes which usually occur singly. Many fine slabs showing several fishes have also been discovered.

The Upper Devonian fish *Eusthenopteron* is known from Europe and North America. Its fins had fleshy bases and it was able to use them to travel over land. The arrangement of bones in the skull is very similar to that of the earliest amphibians, which indicates that *Eusthenopteron* is closely related to the ancestry of land vertebrates.

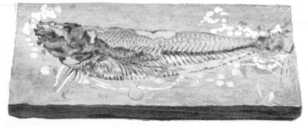

reconstruction
of *Eusthenopteron* Devonian

Scombroclupea Cretaceous

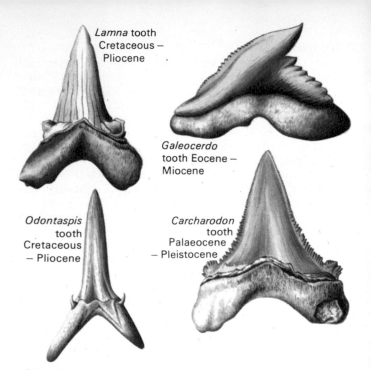

Lamna tooth Cretaceous – Pliocene

Galeocerdo tooth Eocene – Miocene

Odontaspis tooth Cretaceous – Pliocene

Carcharodon tooth Palaeocene – Pleistocene

Sharks and rays

The sharks and rays (class Chondrichthyes) first occur in the Upper Devonian and are therefore the last of the fish classes to appear in the fossil record. They have skeletons that are composed entirely of cartilage, which is a semi-transparent, gristle-like material that decays much more quickly than bone and is therefore rarely fossilized. However, sharks and rays have very hard teeth that are frequently fossilized and are common in many deposits of Carboniferous and later age.

The teeth of sharks grow in rows on the inner sides of the jaws and gradually move into place as earlier teeth become worn or broken and fall out. As a result there is continual replacement of teeth at each position in the jaw. This ensures that the shark always has a working dentition but it also means that during its lifetime each shark may produce thousands of teeth.

Much can be learned about the way of life of a shark or ray from a study of its teeth. Sharks with high, sharply pointed teeth such as *Lamna* and *Odontaspis* were active hunters that caught other fishes.

Those with low, flattened teeth probably fed on molluscs as this type of tooth is suitable for crushing the heavy shells of bivalves. The Mesozoic sharks *Hybodus* and *Acrodus* had numerous, flattened teeth at the back of the jaws while near the front there were many sharp teeth indicating that they could eat a variety of food.

Most of the modern sharks had developed by Cretaceous times and the group changed little during the Caenozoic. One of the most spectacular sharks was *Carcharodon* which occurs in the Tertiary and Pleistocene of Europe. The teeth of *Carcharodon* are up to ten centimetres long which suggests that the shark was as much as twenty metres in length.

Although teeth are the most frequently encountered fossil shark remains, deposits may also include long slender spines that frequently have ornamented surfaces. These are fin spines and in life they supported the fins of certain sharks such as *Acrodus*.

The most specialized mollusc-eating chondrichthyes are the rays. These close relatives of the sharks have evolved very large 'wings' on either side of the body. These are greatly enlarged front fins and are the main organs used in swimming, in contrast to the sharks in which the tail provides the power. Rays are mainly bottom-living fishes and many of them have very large, flattened, plate-like teeth such as those of *Myliobatis,* which is known from Cretaceous and later deposits and survives as the eagle ray.

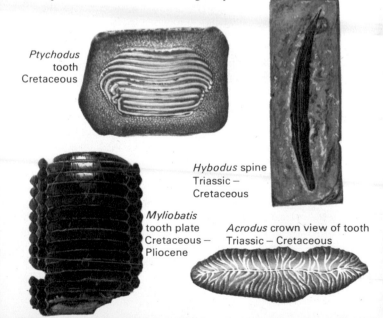

Ptychodus
tooth
Cretaceous

Hybodus spine
Triassic –
Cretaceous

Myliobatis
tooth plate
Cretaceous –
Pliocene

Acrodus crown view of tooth
Triassic – Cretaceous

frog *Rana*
Oligocene
of Spain

Amphibians

Frogs, newts and salamanders are living members of the class Amphibia. They lay their eggs in water – e.g., frog spawn – and have a water-living larval or tadpole stage. Amphibians first occur in the Devonian and they are fairly abundant in Carboniferous rocks. It is assumed that fossil amphibians had moist skins similar to those of a frog, while details of their skulls indicate that they had aquatic larval stages. These features mean that though they could walk on land the amphibians were still dependent on water in which to lay their eggs, and this dependence meant that on land they were much less successful than the reptiles. Carboniferous and Permian amphibians were large and probably lived in swamps. *Eryops* from the Permian of North America was about two metres long.

Frogs and toads are the most successful living amphibians. They have very specialized skeletons with short back bones and very long hind legs which enable them to hop. Frogs probably originated in late Palaeozoic or early Mesozoic times and skeletons of frogs are known from the Jurassic of North America. Many complete skeletons of frogs are known from the Oligocene of Spain and in these the outline of the flesh is indicated around the fossilized bones.

Reptiles

Living reptiles include the snakes, lizards, crocodiles and turtles. Reptiles have scaly skins and they lay eggs. They are cold-blooded and may be distinguished from amphibians and mammals by several features of their skeletons. Fossil reptiles occur in several parts of Britain and Europe and the remains of crocodiles and turtles may be very common in Tertiary deposits.

Flying reptiles

The flying reptiles or pterosaurs were common in the Jurassic and Cretaceous. Early pterosaurs were small but later forms were very large and *Pteranodon* had a wing spread of about eight metres. The pterosaur wing consisted of a sheet of skin supported by a long front limb in which the fourth finger was extremely lengthened. As in the birds, many of the bones were hollow and the large chest bone or sternum indicates the presence of strong flight muscles. The long skull carried beak-like jaws in which there were many small teeth. In *Pteranodon,* the large crest at the back of the skull acted as a rudder, allowing the reptile to control its direction and also keeping the head pointing forwards during flight. The remains of pterosaurs are usually found in marine deposits and they were probably similar to the gulls in their way of life.

Turtles

Turtles and tortoises have very heavy shells or **carapaces** that consist of numerous bony plates or **scutes**. The carapace is fused to

Pteranodon

Pterodactylus

the shoulder and pelvic bones and to the backbone. Most living families of turtles had developed by the end of the Mesozoic and the group was successful throughout the Caenozoic. Fossil turtle scutes are relatively common in freshwater and marine deposits in the Eocene and Oligocene of southern Britain. Scutes with smooth faces are from marine turtles, while those having patterned surfaces are from freshwater turtles, such as *Trionyx* which survives as the snapping turtle.

Crocodiles

Most deposits which contain fossil turtles also include the remains of crocodiles. The alligators and crocodiles are the only reptilian survivors of the great reptile group known as the archosaurs which also includes the dinosaurs, pterosaurs and the ancestors of the birds. Along the top of the skull and the back of the crocodile there is a series of flat plates that have deeply pitted upper surfaces. These plates are common as fossils. Crocodile teeth are also common in Caenozoic freshwater and marine deposits. They are usually conical and may be slightly curved with a pair of strong ridges and numerous fine ridges running along them.

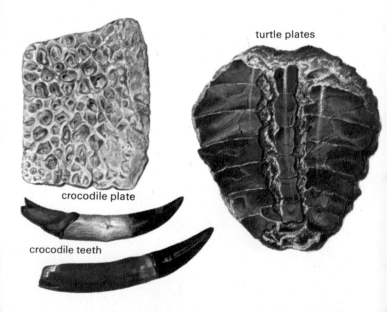

turtle plates

crocodile plate

crocodile teeth

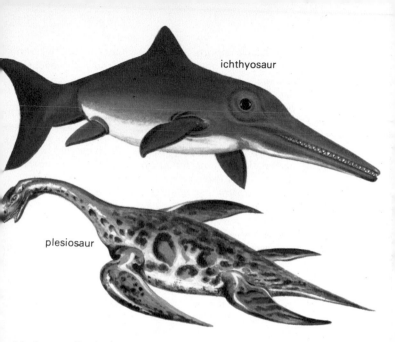

ichthyosaur

plesiosaur

Marine reptiles

Many fossil turtles and some crocodiles were marine but during the Mesozoic the most important marine reptiles were the plesiosaurs and the ichthyosaurs.

Plesiosaurs were usually large, up to fifteen metres long, and they were specialized for marine life, having long necks and well-developed flippers with many small bones in the fingers and toes. Plesiosaurs probably swam in a seal-like manner while the ichthyosaurs swam by using their tails. Ichthyosaurs were fish-like in shape with large flattened tails and a triangular dorsal fin. The limbs were developed as steering fins and the face was very long with many small teeth in the slender jaws. Ichthyosaurs were fully adapted to life in the sea and some complete skeletons contain the remains of baby ichthyosaurs which were born fully developed.

Plesiosaurs are common in the Jurassic of Europe and the Cretaceous of North America. Their fossil remains usually consist of isolated vertebrae, teeth or toe bones, but many complete skeletons have been collected from the Jurassic of Britain. Ichthyosaurs occur mainly in the Triassic and Jurassic and again the remains most frequently encountered are their teeth, vertebrae and toe bones.

Dinosaurs

Dinosaurs first became important in Triassic times. They originated from a reptile group known as the thecodonts (order Thecodontia) that contained small, flesh-eating reptiles which walked using only their hind legs – i.e., they were bipedal. The large, flesh-eating dinosaurs such as *Megalosaurus* and *Tyrannosaurus* also walked on their hind legs and their front limbs were short and weak. *Megalosaurus* occurs in the Jurassic and Cretaceous of Europe and is known from the Jurassic of Britain. The large plant-eating dinosaurs such as *Brontosaurus* are known as sauropods. They are also known from the Jurassic and Cretaceous of Europe and occur in the Cretaceous of Britain. These giant reptiles walked on all four legs and they were the largest land animals that ever lived.

These two dinosaur groups are closely related and are both included in the order Saurischia. The other order of dinosaurs is the Ornithischia and members of the two groups are distinguished by details of their pelvises. The ornithischian dinosaurs were abundant in Cretaceous times and their remains are well known from Europe. *Stegosaurus* was about the size of an elephant, it was quadrupedal and had a row of large flat plates along its back. The remains of *Stegosaurus* have been discovered in Britain but they are very rare. *Iguanodon* is one of the best known European dinosaurs. It is known from complete skeletons discovered in the Cretaceous of south-east England and the Isle of Wight. In Belgium the skeletons of over twenty individuals were found buried together, which suggests that a herd of these dinosaurs was overwhelmed at one time. *Iguanodon* stood about four metres high and was bipedal. It had a large heavy tail and small front limbs.

Most popularly known dinosaurs were very large but many members of the group were no larger than a dog, and *Hypsilophodon* from the Lower Cretaceous of Europe was less than a metre long. A complete skeleton of this bipedal, plant-eating dinosaur was discovered on the Isle of Wight and interpretation of this skeleton suggests that *Hypsilophodon* probably lived and fed among the branches of trees.

The remains of dinosaurs occur in many parts of Europe. They are most common in the Jurassic and Cretaceous of Britain but they are almost always fragmentary, usually consisting of isolated vertebrae, teeth or bone fragments.

Skeleton of *Iguanodon* from the Cretaceous of the Isle of Wight, Britain, and reconstruction.

Birds

Living birds (class: Aves) have feathers and wings, are bipedal and warm-blooded, and lay eggs. They have horny beaks instead of teeth and most birds are able to fly. The mechanical demands of flying have greatly influenced the overall anatomy of the skeleton and soft tissues. To lighten the skeleton the bones are very thin-walled and the larger bones, which are hollow, contain air sacs that communicate with the lungs. The birds originated from the reptiles and their ancestors were probably closely related to the dinosaurs and early crocodiles.

Archaeopteryx is the earliest-known bird. Three skeletons and several less complete specimens of *Archaeopteryx* were discovered during the last century in the Upper Jurassic, Lithographic Limestone of Solnhofen, Germany. The better specimens clearly show the impressions of feathers around the fossil bones. The skull of *Archaeopteryx* is bird-like with a large brain-case and eye sockets, but the jaws carried numerous small teeth which indicates that a beak was not developed. The bones of the wings were relatively short and the fingers were well developed with three claws retained. The bony tail of *Archaeopteryx* was very long and the backbone shows none of the specializations found in later birds. The bones were solid with no sign of the lightening or hollowing that is characteristic of birds. Overall, the skeleton is very similar to that of a small dinosaur, and were it not for the feathers, it is likely that *Archaeopteryx* would have been identified as a reptile. Its small wings, poorly developed breast bone (sternum) and heavy skeleton indicate that *Archaeopteryx* was a weak flier and it probably relied mainly on gliding from tree to tree.

The delicate structure of bird bones means that they are easily broken up and are rare as fossils. In Britain they occur in the Lower Eocene, London Clay deposits and in the Upper Eocene and Oligocene of the Isle of Wight and southern England. These localities have yielded the remains of early grebes, pelicans, ibises and ducks. Fossil birds are also known from many Pleistocene localities in Britain. Fossil bones may be grouped with the birds on the basis of their hollow, thin-walled structure. They are identified by comparison with the skeletons of living birds. This identification is difficult and if you discover the remains of fossil birds in Tertiary deposits you will probably need to take them to a museum for identification.

Reconstruction and fossil specimen of *Archaeopteryx*.

Mammals

All animals that are warm-blooded and have fur are grouped in the class Mammalia. Nearly all members of the class give birth to fully developed young. Mammals have very special cheek teeth and the patterns of cusps, or small lumps, on the cheek teeth is used to identify most fossil mammals. Fossil mammals are generally rare but you may find Eocene or Oligocene mammals in Britain and remains of Pleistocene mammals occur frequently.

Mesozoic mammals

The earliest mammals occur in Upper Triassic rocks. These early mammals are known as pantotheres and a complete skeleton of the pantothere *Megazostrodon* was discovered in 1966 in Lesotho, southern Africa. The limestone hills of south Wales formed islands in the Triassic sea and deep cracks in the limestone became filled with Triassic sediments that included thousands of teeth, jaws and bones of two tiny pantotheres known as *Morganucodon* and *Kuehneotherium*. These were shrew-like mammals with long, slender faces. Their bodies were probably covered with fur and they had high points on their cheek teeth, which indicates that they fed on insects and other small invertebrates. Mammals are also known from the Jurassic (Oxfordshire and Skye) and Lower Cretaceous (Kent) of Europe but only a single tooth is known from the European Upper Cretaceous. In contrast, Upper Cretaceous mammals are common in North America. Most Mesozoic mammals were small and shrew-like, none being larger than a dog.

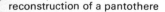

reconstruction of a pantothere

Reconstruction of *Palaeotherium*. This relative of the horse lived in southern England and Europe in Eocene times, about forty-five million years ago.

Palaeocene and Eocene mammals

When the dinosaurs became extinct at the end of the Mesozoic they left the way open for the mammals to become dominant on land. This they did very quickly and the Tertiary is often known as 'The Age of Mammals'. Palaeocene mammals are unknown from Britain and are rare from the rest of Europe with the richest localities in France. Eocene mammals are far more common and are well known from the London and Paris basins and from Hampshire and the Isle of Wight. The Lower Eocene mammals of the London Clay include *Hyracotherium* which is the ancestor of the horses and is also known from the Palaeocene and Eocene of North America (p. 20).

The Upper Eocene clays and limestones of southern Hampshire and the Isle of Wight contain the remains of primates, rodents, shrews, opossums, carnivorous mammals and other early relatives of the horses known as *Plagiolophus* and *Palaeotherium*. These were large, tapir-like mammals that inhabited the warm swampy forests growing in southern Britain during late Eocene times. These deposits are the richest collecting areas for British Tertiary mammals and over the last few years they have yielded many thousands of teeth and bones of small mammals.

Oligocene mammals

By Oligocene times mammalian faunas were beginning to develop a modern aspect. Almost all of the mammalian orders are known from the Oligocene and many modern mammalian families were in existence. Oligocene mammals are very well known from Europe, North America and north Africa. These faunas show great differences which indicates that these regions were isolated from one another. Oligocene rocks of Wyoming, Nebraska and South Dakota contain the richest known deposits of Tertiary mammals and have yielded a fauna that includes early dogs, sabre-toothed cats, relatives of the rabbits, several rodents, rhinoceroses, three-toed horses and huge titanotheres, which were almost as big as elephants and had great forked horns on their noses. The Oligocene fauna of Libya and Egypt includes the earliest elephants (*Palaeomastodon*) as well as whales, seacows, hyraxes and primates.

Oligocene deposits on the Isle of Wight have also yielded a large fauna of fossil mammals. The deposits suggest warm climatic conditions with dense forest vegetation. *Bothriodon* was a large pig-like mammal that lived along the banks of rivers and streams and fed on soft aquatic vegetation. The opossum *Peratherium* also occurs and is the only marsupial (pouched mammal) known from Europe. Living marsupials include the opossum, kangaroo and wombat. The group originated in the Americas and marsupials reached Australia in early Tertiary times. They survived in North America until the Miocene and reached Europe in Eocene times but became extinct here in the Oligocene.

The hornless rhinoceros *Ronzotherium* is well known from the European Oligocene and is represented by a few teeth and bones from the Isle of Wight. Rodents are very common in the Isle of Wight deposits and during the last few years several thousand teeth have been collected by careful sieving of the deposits. The lemur-like primate *Adapis* is also known. These plant-eating mammals probably provided the food for the flesh-eating *Hyaenodon*, which was about the sixe of a large dog and was similar in its way of life to the living hyaena or lion. The Isle of Wight deposits are the richest source of Tertiary mammal remains in Britain and they contain a fauna that is very similar to the much larger and richer deposits at Quercy in France which have yielded hundreds of complete skeletons and skulls of the European Oligocene mammals.

Reconstruction of an Isle of Wight scene in the Oligocene. **Key:** a *Adapis*, b *Xiphodon*, c *Ronzotherium*, d *Bothriodon*, e *Hyaenodon*.

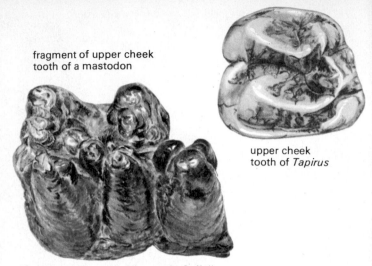

fragment of upper cheek
tooth of a mastodon

upper cheek
tooth of *Tapirus*

Fossil teeth from the Pliocene in Suffolk.

Miocene and Pliocene mammals

The Miocene and Pliocene saw great changes in the mammalian fauna of Europe as modern forms increased in importance at the expense of more primitive genera. Modern types of flesh-eating mammals such as cats and dogs (order Carnivora) were now dominant while the primitive flesh-eaters (order Creodonta) became extinct, although they survived in Asia until the Pliocene. Deer and antelopes expanded while rhinoceroses and mastodons were among the larger, plant-eating mammals. Towards the end of the Miocene, advanced three-toed horses reached Eurasia from North America while giraffes, early sheep, goats, gazelles, antelopes, cats, hyaenas and a host of smaller mammals are known from the very rich deposits of Pikermi near Athens and the island of Samos. At this time a huge belt of grassland stretched across Asia and Europe from China to France and North Africa. This grassland carried a mammalian fauna that was similar in structure to the present fauna of southern Africa, and demonstrated the condition of the mammals when they were probably at the peak of their development. The Miocene and Pliocene climatic conditions seem to have favoured the expansion of the mammals but the end of the Pliocene saw a rapid deterioration in climate, and since then many genera and families of mammals have become extinct.

The Pleistocene

The Pleistocene period occupies about two million years and ended about 10 000 years ago. During this time great climatic changes occurred which had a profound effect upon the vegetation and fauna of the world and vastly altered the landscape of the northern countries. At least three times the North Polar ice cap expanded in size, sweeping southwards as a vast ice sheet which at its maximum extent covered most of northern Europe and in Britain reached as far south as a line running from Bristol to the Wash. Periods when the ice sheets were large are known as *glacial periods* and at these times the climate of Europe was extremely cold. At the same time so much water was tied up in the ice that sea-levels changed throughout the world with the bed of the English Channel and parts of the North Sea occurring as dry land. When the ice was at its maximum southern extent it is unlikely that there were any mammals in Britain but during the cold climatic conditions of glacial periods, fossil evidence indicates a cold weather fauna with woolly mammoths (*Mammuthus*), woolly rhinoceroses (*Coelodonta*), bears, polar bears, reindeer, wolves, lemmings and wolverines all represented. Overall, the British countryside and part of the fauna resembled that of modern northern Canada or Siberia.

woolly mammoth

woolly rhinoceros

giant deer

straight-tusked
elephant

hyaena   sabre-toothed cat

Periods when the ice sheets had retreated are known as *inter-glacials*. In these times relatively warm conditions existed and a correspondingly warm-weather type of fauna was present, with straight-tusked elephants, rhinoceroses, hyaenas, lions, sabre-toothed cats, horses, giant deer (*Megaloceros*) and monkeys all known from Britain, while hippopotamuses were common in the south and extended as far northwards as the Yorkshire moors.

These climatic changes during the Ice Ages occurred gradually over several tens of thousands of years and there is no evidence to indicate that the Ice Ages are over. We may now be living in what is just another interglacial period and in perhaps another 100 000 years the ice sheets may once again move southwards to begin another glacial period.

Man reached Britain about one quarter of a million years ago and the earliest known human remains in this country occur at Swans-combe in Kent. Man's influence on the mammalian fauna has been very great and those mammals that survive are a poor reflection of the fauna that existed as late as 1 000 years ago.

FOSSIL PLANTS

Fossil plants may be very abundant in restricted areas but overall they are much rarer than fossil animals. The plants form the other major kingdom of living organisms. Most plants contain a green substance known as chlorophyll which enables them to produce food materials known as carbohydrates – e.g., starch – by a chemical process involving water and carbon dioxide and using sunlight as the source of energy. This process is known as photosynthesis and is of fundamental importance to life on earth because plants are at the bases of all animal food chains. Also, animals take in oxygen and after respiration they give out carbon dioxide, whereas during photosynthesis plants take in carbon dioxide and release oxygen. Thus plants help maintain a balance between the amounts of these two gases in the atmosphere.

The algae are amongst the simplest plants. They are all aquatic and the group includes the seaweeds and some of the slimy green plants found in freshwater. Remains of algae are known from rocks of Precambrian (p. 29) and later age but their identification involves the study and interpretation of thin sections and is not covered here. Liverworts and mosses are slightly more advanced plants but both are rare as fossils.

Early plants

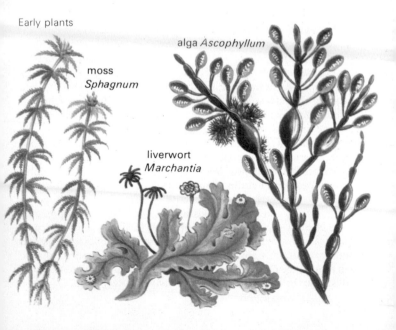

moss
Sphagnum

alga *Ascophyllum*

liverwort
Marchantia

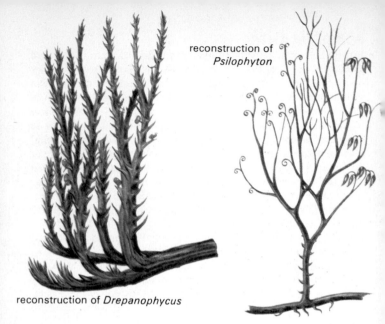

reconstruction of *Psilophyton*

reconstruction of *Drepanophycus*

Early land plants

A group of very simple plants known as the psilopsids (order Psilophytales) represent the earliest stages of the colonization of land by the plants and their fossil remains occur in the Upper Silurian of Australia and the Devonian of North America and Europe. One of the most famous of these fossil floras is from the Middle Devonian of Rhynie near Aberdeen in Scotland where there is a concentration of fossilized plants very like a peat bed.

The commonest plant in the Rhynie flora is *Psilophyton* which had a creeping underground stem known as a rhizome. From this there grew erect forking shoots. Many of the smaller branches had double tips with each part curling back on itself, while at the tips of some branches there were oval reproductive bodies that produced spores.

Psilophyton and similar forms such as *Drepanophycus* represent a stage of plant evolution before structures such as true roots, leaves or seeds had developed. The cells in the stem had different functions with the central few providing support while the outer ones conducted sap around the plant. This and the branching and leaf-like structures constitute the basic essentials for life on land.

Coal-measure plants

Much of our information about early plants comes from study of the huge fossil floras known from the coal measures of the world. By the Carboniferous, plants were well established on land and huge forests occupied much of what is now Britain, the bed of the North Sea and Europe, and these forests contained a wealth of different plants.

Scale trees and club mosses

The living club mosses such as *Lycopodium* are small, herbaceous plants in which the stem and branches are covered with small, elongate leaves. They are included in a group of spore-bearing plants known as the lycopsids which were at the peak of their development during Carboniferous times when they were represented by the scale trees such as *Lepidodendron* and *Sigillaria*. These were the commonest and most spectacular of the coal-measure plants and some scale trees were up to forty-five metres high.

The trunks and branches of the lycopods increased in thickness by the addition of layers of wood around the outer region, as in modern trees, and the young trunk and branches had dense coverings of leaves that had a spiral arrangement in *Lepidodendron* but were vertically arranged in *Sigillaria*. In older parts of the plant these leaves were lost but their attachment scars remained throughout the

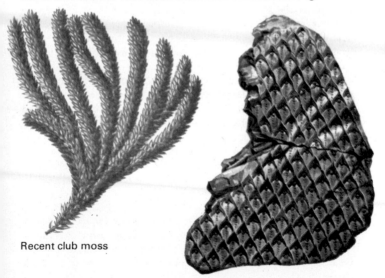

Recent club moss

piece of *Lepidodendron* showing leaf scars

life of the tree. The different parts of the scale trees are usually found separately and as a result they have been given different names. Thus the names *Lepidodendron* and *Sigillaria* are applied to the trunk of the scale tree while *Stigmaria* is applied to the roots and *Lepidostrobus* refers to the spore-producing structures.

Horsetails and tree ferns

The living horsetails or scouring rushes (*Equisetum*) represent the last survivors of the sphenopsids which formed an important Palaeozoic group of spore-bearing plants. Sphenopsids are character-ized by their jointed stems on which the leaves, shoots and branches are produced only at the joints. The stem was hollow and fossil sphenopsids frequently consist only of internal moulds of the stem. One of the commonest Carboniferous sphenopsids was *Calamites* which may have been as much as twelve metres tall. The leaves of sphenopsids were carried in whorls – e.g., *Annularia* – and the reproductive structures were cone-like and produced spores – e.g., *Calamostachys*.

Ferns and seed ferns

The living ferns reproduce by means of spores and many Car-boniferous plants such as *Ptychocarpus* are closely related to the living ferns and also reproduced by spores. Members of a second group of fern-like plants – the Pteridospermae – reproduced by means of seeds. It is usually necessary for the seed- or spore-producing structure to be preserved for an expert to distinguish easily ferns from seed ferns.

Neuropteris is a seed fern having elongate, almost oval leaves that are arranged in pairs along the stem with the single seed developing at the tip of the stem. *Ptychocarpus* has very small leaves and spore-bearing bodies have been found in some specimens which indicates that it is a true fern. The true ferns and seed ferns probably evolved from a common ancestor during the Devonian. True ferns have been successful since the Palaeozoic but the seed ferns became extinct at some time in the Mesozoic.

Finding fossil plants in coal

The fossil remains of plants are particularly common in coal and the best place to search for them is on the tip heaps near coal mines. Flattened leaves often occur along bedding planes but it is worth-while splitting open nodules as they may contain leaves or cone-like fossils.

Neuropteris leaves

reconstruction of *Lepidodendron*

Annularia leaves

Ptychocarpus leaves

Calamites stem

reconstruction of *Calamites*

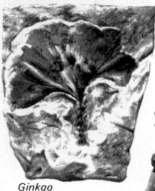

Ginkgo
leaf Jurassic – Recent

Cordaianthus
cone Carboniferous

Cordaites
leaf fragment
Carboniferous

Conifers

The living cone-bearing trees such as the pine, fir and redwood have a good fossil record extending as far back as the Upper Carboniferous and the group began to expand rapidly in importance in early Mesozoic times, while pines are known to have existed as long ago as Jurassic times and all the living families of conifers are known throughout the Caenozoic. One of the most primitive of the living conifers is the monkey puzzle tree (*Araucaria*) and cones very similar to those of the monkey puzzle tree are known from the Triassic of South America (*Proaraucaria*). The conifers originated from a group of large forest-living trees belonging to the group Cordaitales which includes the genus *Cordaites*. The leaves of *Cordaites* were up to one metre long and were strap-like with ridges running along them. Cones of the genus *Cordaianthus* had a very open structure which is typical of all members of the Cordaitales.

The ginkgo

The living ginkgo or maidenhair tree is the last remaining species (*Ginkgo biloba*) of a group of trees that were common in the Mesozoic and Caenozoic. Leaves of the ginkgo are fan-shaped and characteristically consist of two lobes with the veins running along them.

The earliest-known plants that carried flower-like structures are the Bennetitales which range from the Carboniferous to Cretaceous and are represented by *Williamsonia* which had a disc-like male flower that was divided into petal-like stamens in its upper region. The Bennetitales are not, however, regarded as true flowering plants.

Flowering plants

The flowering plants or angiosperms form by far the most important and abundant group of living plants. All angiosperms reproduce by means of seeds which are enclosed by protective coatings. Details of the seeds are important for understanding the main subdivisions of the angiosperms. If you take a bean and strip off its outer skin you will find that the seed consists of two disc-like pieces that are easily separated and have only a very small region where they are joined. These two pieces are really modified leaves and are called **cotyledons**. In beans, peas, acorns, chestnuts and a host of other seeds there are two cotyledons and this group of flowering plants is called the **dicotyledons**. If you take a grain of maize or barley you will find that it consists of a single cotyledon and the group of plants that has seeds like this is called the **monocotyledons**.

Williamsonia
Triassic –
Cretaceous

grass

oak leaf Pleistocene

Although details of the seeds provide the key to identifying a plant as a monocot or dicot there are several other differences between members of these two groups. In dicots the leaves are usually wide with a net-like pattern of veins. Also, in a cross-section of the stem the vascular bundles are restricted to the outer region. In contrast, in the monocots the veins of the leaf run parallel to each other along the length of the leaf as in grass and the vascular bundles are distributed throughout the cross-section of the stem.

There are well over 30 000 known species of fossil angiosperms ranging from the Lower Cretaceous. Leaves, flowers, fruits and wood occur and details of any part may be used for identification. The fossil record shows that the flowering plants expanded rapidly during the Cretaceous, and by the end of the Mesozoic they were well established with a worldwide distribution. Many surviving families were already in existence including the Fagaceae which contains the oak and beech, the Magnoliaceae which includes the magnolias, the Saleaceae which includes the willow and poplar, and the palms.

Fossil plants from the Caenozoic are very useful in the study of past climates. The earliest angiosperms were trees, with herbaceous forms developing later, and most living kinds of forest trees are

Left Polished cross-section of oak *Quercus*, Eocene – Recent.
Right Polished cross-section of palm *Palmoxylon*, Cretaceous – Recent.

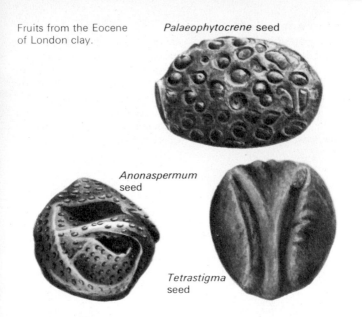

Fruits from the Eocene of London clay.

Palaeophytocrene seed

Anonaspermum seed

Tetrastigma seed

known by the Miocene. This allows deductions to be made about past climates by comparing the compositions of fossil floras with those of modern floras. Such comparisons indicate the existence of comparatively mild conditions in Antarctica during Cretaceous times when members of the Fagaceae grew there, while a large fossil flora of over 200 species from the Cretaceous of Greenland includes poplars, beech, cinnamon, plane and heather.

One of the most famous and important Lower Tertiary floras is that of the London Clay deposits that are early Eocene in age. The London Clay flora contains the leaves, fruits and wood of over 300 species. During the early Eocene a large river flowed south-east-wards across Britain and emptied into the sea near London, while marine currents from the north-east caused floating debris to accumulate near what is now the Isle of Sheppey. As a result the deposits of London Clay on the Isle of Sheppey, Kent are very rich in fossil-plant remains. These fossils are not usually found in the clay but on the shore where the sea washes away the soft clay and mud, and leaves the harder, heavier, fossil-plant remains. Wave action then concentrates this material into small pockets on the shore.

Pollen analysis

Pollen analysis is one of the most important contributions made by palaeobotany to studies of stratigraphy and past environments. These techniques are of particular importance in the study of Tertiary and Pleistocene rocks and have provided particularly important information on events during the Ice Ages.

Pollen is produced by seed bearing plants only and each grain of pollen has an outer wall that is resistant to decay and is therefore easily fossilized. Pollen grains will, however, oxidize relatively

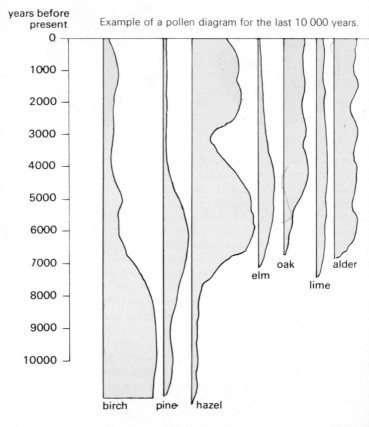

Example of a pollen diagram for the last 10 000 years.

% of tree pollen in samples

quickly if exposed to the air and pollen is best preserved under water, either in marshes, lakes or the sea. The richest pollen samples are usually collected from peat. Pollen must be studied under a microscope and different species of plants may be identified from the appearance of their pollen grains.

Pollen analysis involves the study of pollen from progressively younger deposits in sequence. In this technique, the pollen grains within samples are counted and the plants to which they belong are identified. From this the relative abundance of plant species in the fossil flora can be assessed and by studying samples in sequence, progressive changes in floras can be discovered. These changes will reflect either changes in climate or changes in the condition of the surrounding land.

The ratios of different plant species in the deposits, as revealed by pollen counts, are usually plotted graphically in the form of a *pollen diagram* such as the one shown. This demonstrates that in the area studied birch woodland was particularly important about 10 000 years ago but over the next few thousand years there were progressive changes with pine and hazel becoming important before the appearance of oak and elm, and eventually the establishment of mixed oak woodland. This sequence reflects gradual changes in the climate since the last Ice Age with the birch indicating relatively cold conditions and the mixed woodland indicating conditions similar to those of today.

Pollen analysis is also widely used in archaeology as changes in the relative importance of certain plants such as cereals are reflected in the pollen diagrams and clearly indicate the changes produced in the flora by the development of agriculture.

Although of particular importance in studies of Caenozoic and Recent environments, pollen analysis has also been applied to some Mesozoic and even Palaeozoic rocks. If the study of fossil spores is included loosely under the term pollen analysis then the technique has application as far back as the Silurian, from which the earliest known spores have been discovered in rocks about 400 million years old.

The study of Pleistocene and more recent pollen is relatively easy for the expert as he can compare the pollen directly with that of living plant species. However, pollen analysis becomes increasingly difficult in older rocks as extinct species and even whole extinct groups of plants may be represented by pollen which cannot be associated with fossilized wood, leaves, or flowers to allow identification.

COLLECTING FOSSILS

The best areas in which to collect are quarries, cliffs, road cuttings and tip heaps from mines, while the beds and banks of rivers often have good collecting possibilities. Before entering quarries that are still being worked you must always obtain permission. This usually requires a visit to the quarry office and in Britain you may be asked to sign a form which releases the quarry owners from legal responsibility for your safety. When collecting on farm land it is as well to

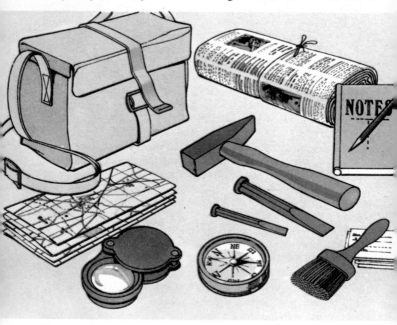

Some useful collecting equipment.

ask the farmer's permission. In both quarries and farms, time used obtaining permission is usually well spent because quarry workers or farmers often know the areas where you will find the best specimens. When collecting on agricultural land you should keep to pathways, or if these are absent walk around the edges of fields, especially if they are ploughed or have growing crops in them. Never leave litter, avoid livestock and always close gates after you.

It is quite possible to collect fossils without using any special

first find the specimen

remove it carefully from the rock

take notes

wrap to carry it home

number the specimen

equipment but if you intend to collect at all seriously than a few things will make your work much more comfortable and rewarding. Stout shoes or boots, heavy denim jeans and an anorak are the main special clothes needed and you probably own these already. For the actual collecting you will need a geological hammer. At least two cold chisels, one large and one small, will be useful. Other equipment consists of several small boxes, lots of newspaper, string, a tape measure and a compass, a lens, a notebook, a pen that uses waterproof ink, road maps, a geological map of the area and if available a geological guide to the area. If you own a camera you may find it useful to provide yourself with a pictorial record of your collecting. To carry all this equipment and your fossils you will need a stout canvas rucksack.

Let us suppose that you have found a specimen in a quarry. It may be possible to break off the rock that contains it, using the blunt head of the geological hammer, or to split the rock using the sharp or chisel edge of the hammer. Failing this you should use the hammer and one of the chisels to cut around the specimen, keeping well away from it to avoid chipping or flaking. When you have removed the specimen with its attached rock, write an identification number on it using the waterproof ink. A good method of identification numbering is based on the date. Thus 3975/4/12 would mean that the specimen was collected on the third (3) of September (9), 1975. It was found at the fourth locality visited (4) and was the twelfth specimen found in that locality (12). Alternatively you may keep a list of your localities which will then be numbered independently. In your notebook you will record the identification along with notes that you think relevant to the specimen, such as its exact position in the quarry, its orientation, height on the rock face, other specimens found at the same level, etc. The notebook is also useful for recording details of the localities, such as means of access, name and address of the landowner, where the nearest cafe is and so on. Such useful details may make later visits easier.

Having completed your notes, wrap the specimen in newspaper and tie it as a parcel. Small specimens should be wrapped in tissue and placed in one of your boxes. The maps and guide will be useful to find collecting localities and to find your position in the geological sequence. In the case of well-known localities the guide will probably give details and notes on the rocks and fossils to be found.

Remember that complete specimens may be extremely rare. When you first arrive it is as well to collect any fragments that are identifiable; you can always sort out and reject poorer specimens later.

Also, there will be specimens that you cannot remove from rocks or cliff faces – do not destroy them, someone else may be able to remove them or they may weather out slowly.

To find specimens over about half a centimetre in diameter, no one has yet devised a collecting method much better than looking over the rock surface. Do not be afraid to crawl with your eyes only about twenty centimetres (one foot) from the ground. This method

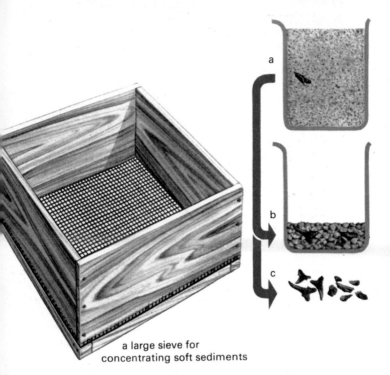

a large sieve for concentrating soft sediments

Sieving for fossils. **Key: a** the sediment as it occurs naturally; **b** after concentration in the sieve, most particles are the same size; **c** the specimens are then picked from the concentrate.

also works very well for smaller specimens that are present in very low concentrations in the deposits.

With very small specimens, that are present in clays or sands, sieving techniques work very well. You can make sieves, similar to the one shown, for a few pounds each, but in really rich deposits an old kitchen sieve is very effective. The mesh of the sieve must be smaller than the specimens you are trying to collect. With clays, the sediment should be dried thoroughly either in strong sunlight or in an oven. This helps break down the clay particles. The sediment is placed in the sieves and either shaken dry or placed in water and shaken so that small particles pass through the mesh and the particles that you are interested in are concentrated in the sieve. You will find by experience whether it is better to sieve the sediments dry or under water. Clays will require several washings and dryings to completely remove the small particles. The concentrate can then be 'picked' either with the naked eye if the fossils are relatively large, or under a microscope for smaller specimens.

Preparation

When you have collected your specimens and carried them home they will probably need preparation and the method that you use for this will depend on the type of fossils and the rock in which they are enclosed. Fossils in clay should be dried thoroughly and then soaked in water for several hours. The drying and soaking will cause the clay to break down and complete specimens may then be washed out. Mechanical preparation techniques involve the scraping or chipping away of the surrounding rock. Three items of equipment useful for this are a small steel chisel, a small hammer and a pin vice. The first two are easily obtainable but the last will only be found in good hardware stores. Pin vices are fairly cheap and they hold disposable steel points. Alternatively a large pin or needle may be used. Mechanical preparation techniques work well with soft rocks such as most chalks, some limestones and sandstones. Using the pin vice or some other sharp steel point, pick at the rock or push the point into the rock at regular intervals about half a centimetre from the surface of the specimen. As you undercut the surrounding rock it can be removed with the hammer and chisel but remember to always strike away from the specimen.

Mechanical methods such as this should also be used for fossils in clay if you can see that they are broken, as soaking will only release the pieces and you may not be able to join them together again.

When preparing many fossils in harder rock you may chip away the surrounding rock with the hammer and chisel. Again the rock will usually flake away from the surface of the fossil but the danger of breaking the specimen is much greater.

Acid techniques

Acid techniques are very important for removing specimens from some harder rocks but before starting any work with acids you must remember that they are dangerous. If you are at school or college ask your chemistry teacher for advice. Acid burns in a chemical way that is not like burning from a flame but is just as serious. Should you get acid on your clothes or skin, soak it off in water for several minutes. Dilute acids will not burn immediately but they will as the water evaporates from them, so speed in removing the acid is important.

Before applying acid techniques it is as well to test the acid on a fragment of the fossil that you intend to prepare, to check that it will not damage the fossil while acting on the rock. Fossil invertebrates that have been impregnated with silica are usually hard and shiny. These fossils can be removed from calcareous rocks such as chalk or limestone by using dilute hydrochloric acid (less than ten per cent) which will attack the rock but has less effect on the fossil. With vertebrate remains, a weak solution of acetic acid (ten to fifteen per cent) should be used. This attacks the calcareous rocks but has no effect on the calcium phosphate content of the bone. It may, however, remove impregnating minerals and therefore make the fossil more fragile. Acids should be used in glass or plastic containers and, since fumes are produced, they should be placed either outside in the garden or in a draughty garden shed, but not in the house. Acid preparation of a specimen may take several weeks as the surface will be exposed only very gradually.

Specimens that have been in contact with salt-water should be soaked in freshwater for several days to remove the salt which will otherwise crystallize inside the specimen and cause damage. This also applies to specimens prepared with acid which should always be soaked for a long period – up to two weeks – with several changes of water, after acid preparation is complete.

With acid techniques and mechanical methods the exposed surface of the fossil should be coated regularly with a plastic-based glue which will protect the fossil, and if sufficiently dilute will impregnate the specimen and make it much stronger. These glues give off inflammable vapours so again care is needed.

There will be some rocks or concretions that cannot be removed with acid and which are difficult to remove by mechanical methods. You will get to know these by experience and will probably find that it is as well to leave these specimens as they are and be satisfied with what is naturally exposed.

Acid preparation of fossils.

rock with only fragments
of bone showing

rock in acid

Acid

With all preparation techniques patience is essential. Should the mechanical preparation be rushed or stronger solutions of acid be used, damage to the specimen will probably result.

Building a collection

Your collection will grow rapidly as you visit rich collecting areas and as your experience of collecting and preparation increases. If you have spent your time on collecting, then your specimens will be valuable to you and you will want to care for them. Specimens can be housed in boxes but a small chest of drawers or a set of shallow

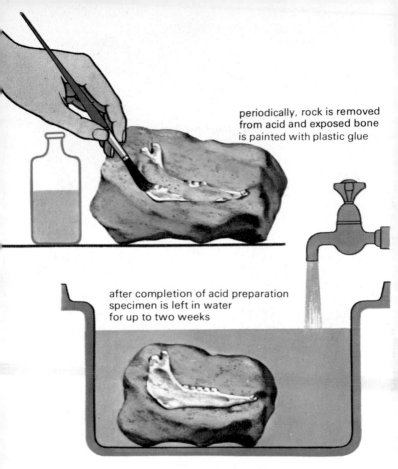

periodically, rock is removed
from acid and exposed bone
is painted with plastic glue

after completion of acid preparation
specimen is left in water
for up to two weeks

trays is preferable. The storage method is a matter of choice but is governed by what you can afford. The order in which you arrange your specimens is also a matter of choice. You may choose to keep all the specimens belonging to one natural group together, so that in one part of your collection there will be all the ammonites while in another there will be all the brachiopods and so on. This arrangement agrees with that used in the main part of this book and will be suitable if you are interested in the groups and changes that occurred in their members with time. Alternatively, the specimens may be stored according to their age or according to the area in which they

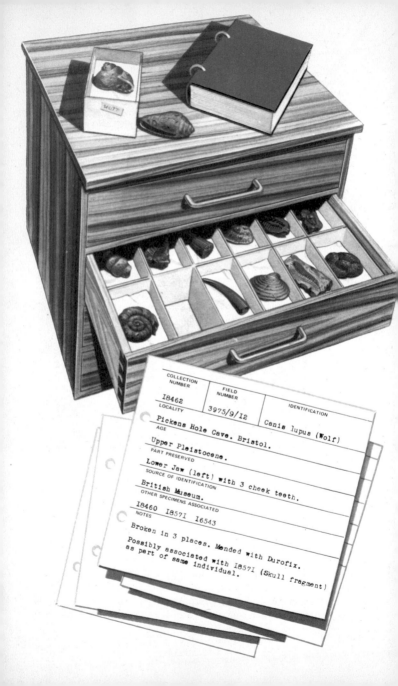

COLLECTION NUMBER	FIELD NUMBER	IDENTIFICATION
I8462	3975/9/I2	Canis lupus (Wolf)

LOCALITY

Pickens Hole Cave. Bristol.

AGE

Upper Pleistocene.

PART PRESERVED

Lower Jaw (left) with 3 cheek teeth.

SOURCE OF IDENTIFICATION

British Museum.

OTHER SPECIMENS ASSOCIATED

I8460 I857I I6543

NOTES

Broken in 3 places. Mended with Durofix.

Possibly associated with I857I (Skull fragment) as part of same individual.

were collected. This method will suit you if you are interested in the ages of the rocks in your collecting areas and in the make up of each fauna or flora during different geological periods.

Before placing specimens in your collection you should identify them. This may be done by comparing the specimens with good figures in text books. If you know the locality from which your specimen came and you know the age of the rocks in which you were collecting, then identification is easier, as there will probably have been only a limited number of species, from each family or class, occurring in any area during one geological period. In many cases local geological guides will list the species known from your collecting localities. Many museums display the commoner species that you may collect from their region but very few museums even attempt to give a wider coverage. As a last resort the geology departments of colleges or museums may identify difficult specimens for you, but remember that you should approach them only in exceptional cases and usually these places will not willingly identify large collections.

When you have prepared and identified your specimen it will be ready for entering into your collection. You may write the identification on the specimen, which is alright as long as the identification is correct, but is difficult to alter if you have made a mistake. It is better to give the specimen a number. This may be the same as your field number (p.112) or you may wish to give it a collection number. You should write out a small card on which there will be the collection number and your identification. You may also wish to insert other details such as the locality and age. This small card should accompany the specimen in your collection. You should also make out a larger card giving full details of the specimen and carrying any other information that you think is important. This card should be filed away in a card index.

Summary

To summarize the total sequence. You must first find the specimen, give it a field number and record details in your field note book. When you get home the specimen should be prepared, identified and given a collection number if this differs from the field number. You then make out a small card and a larger collection card. The collection card is filed and the specimen, with its small card, is placed in your collection.

An example of a storage cabinet for fossils, and a sample record card.

Museums

Museums can be a great source of entertainment and information for you as you build your collection. In a good museum display you will see many excellent fossils, together with reconstructions of the animals or plants that they represent. There may be displays of complete fossil faunas, or displays giving fossils from each geological period. The exhibits will also contain much information about the specimens shown. Visits to museums will therefore assist you in understanding your existing collection. It is also a good idea to visit the local museum before you begin collecting in an area, as the displays will probably show you the kinds of fossils that you can expect to find and may also show the types of rocks in which they occur. When you visit a museum you will see the security staff or guards and you may see members of the education department who give guided lectures and information, but there are also many members of the museum staff who work behind the scenes and who you will never see.

The varied functions of a large museum. **Key: a** scientific research; **b** preparation of reconstructions for display and as an aid to research; **c** care of collections and preparation of new specimens; **d** public displays of good, interesting specimens; **e** storage of large collections; **f** education.

The geology department of a major museum will have a very large collection of fossils which are cared for by geologists known as **curators**. It is their job to collect specimens, identify them, record the details and enter them into the collections. They also care for the collection, keeping the information contained in it up to date and checking enquiries from research workers or other collectors. This is part of their function but the curators probably also do research on part of the collection, or on selected groups of fossil animals or plants. They will also provide information to members of the 'display' or 'exhibition' department, whose job it is to design and construct the displays that you see. This department will include designers, artists, modellers, taxidermists and carpenters.

The fossils in the museum's collection will also be cared for by a group of scientists known as **preparators** or **conservators**. These people are experts in the preparation and treatment of fossils and they may also be involved with making casts of outstanding specimens for exchange, display or research.

The collections of fossils in our large museums are part of the nation's resources and wealth. They are very important for research purposes and are treated with extreme care by those responsible for them.

GLOSSARY

absolute age age of a rock or fossil measured in years before the present

amber fossil resin

aperture opening of gastropod shell

area flattened region of shell between hinge and beak (bivalve mollusc)

auricles wing-like growths of shell, in front and behind the beak (some scallops)

axial structure central structure in corallite (corals)

basal plates lower plates of theca that attach to stem (sea lilies and blastoids)

beak pointed or rounded region near hinge-line in bivalve molluscs and brachiopods

bipedal walking on two feet (e.g., birds and man)

branching plant-like growth form (corals)

carapace shell of turtle or tortoise

carbonization fossilization method in which only the carbon content of the original organism is preserved.

cardinal region part of shell immediately below beak (bivalve molluscs)

cartilage gristle-like substance forming skeleton (sharks and rays)

cephalon head region of trilobite

columella central column of shell (gastropods)

conispiral coiling method in which whorls rise from aperture to form cone (gastropods)

corallite solitary coral or individual of colony

cotyledons fleshy parts of seeds

cusps swellings on crowns of teeth (mammals)

deltoid plates upper thecal plates (blastoids)

dextral coiling in which aperture is on right when apex points upwards (gastropods)

dicots plants in which seeds consist of two cotyledons

dissepiments minor horizontal to vertical divisions of corallites (corals)

encrusting moss-like growth form (corals and bryozoans)

exoskeleton hard outer coating of body in crustaceans etc.

facial suture paired grooves running from front to back on the heads of many trilobites

gape part of shell that has flexed margins and therefore stays permanently open (bivalve molluscs)

genal angle outer back region of head in trilobites

glabella central swelling of head in trilobites

glacial period time when ice sheets were extending southwards during Ice Ages

Gondwanaland southern land mass that existed before the formation of modern continents and consisted of Africa, Australia, South America and Antarctica

hinge line region along which valves articulate (bivalve molluscs and brachiopods)

inequivalve with one valve larger than the other (brachiopods and some bivalve molluscs)

interarea flattened region of shell between hinge line and beak in brachiopods

interglacial period warm time when ice sheets had retreated northwards during Ice Ages

keel ridge along outer face of ammonite

Laurasia northern land mass existing before the formation of modern continents and consisting of Europe, Asia and North America. *See* Gondwanaland and Pangaea

lobe backward projection of suture line (ammonites)

lophophore internal branching structure of brachiopod

massive growth form in which clumps or thick, solid masses are developed (corals and bryozoans)

monocots plants in which seeds have only a single cotyledon

moss animals bryozoans

mould fossil resulting from the filling in of a cavity left after organic remains have decayed or dissolved away

nema attachment thread of graptolite colony

notochord stiffening rod along back, present in the development of all chordates

Pangaea land mass that existed before Gondwanaland and Laurasia had separated

pedicle muscular attachment organ of brachiopod

pendent having branches hanging downwards (graptolites)

pentaradial symmetry body arrangement based on five-rayed plan (echinoderms)

petrifaction fossilization method in which animal or plant remains are impregnated with minerals that increase their hardness and weight

phragmocone hollow region at front end of belemnite

pinnules small hair-like processes on arms of sea lilies

planispiral coiling with mid-lines of whorls all in the same plane (ammonites and gastropods)

pleural regions side regions of trilobites

polyp soft parts of coral animal

pygidium tail region of trilobite

radial plates upper thecal plates (sea lilies); central or side plates (blastoids)

ramp flattened region between shoulder and suture (gastropod)

replacement fossilization method in which original organic remains are replaced by minerals

rostrum bullet-shaped part of belemnite

saddle forward projection of suture line in ammonite

scandent with branches growing upwards (graptolites)

sculpturing grooves, ridges, tubercles or swellings of shell surface

scutes bony plates forming carapace in turtles

seam line along which whorls meet in ammonites

selenizone ridge in sculpturing produced during the growth of some gastropods and indicating the presence of a 'slit' in outer edge of aperture

septum vertical division of corallite (coral); wall dividing chambers (ammonites)

shoulder strong swelling of shell near suture (gastropods)

sinistral coiling in which aperture is on left when apex points upwards (gastropods)

siphuncle narrow tube running through each chamber of ammonite

slit deep notch in outer lip of aperture in some gastropods

spicules skeletal elements composed of silica (sponges, sea cucumbers and starfishes)

stipe branch of graptolite colony

strata layers of rock

suture line along which whorls join (gastropods); region where septum meets wall of shell (ammonites)

tabulae horizontal divisions of corallites (corals)

test hard outer body wall (sea urchins and sea lilies)

trace fossil fossil giving indirect evidence of life (e.g., worm casts, footprints, burrows)

umbilicus depression in base of gastropod or side of ammonite

venter outer edge of ammonite shell

whorl single turn of shell (gastropods)

BOOKS TO READ

British Palaeozoic Fossils (1969), *British Mesozoic Fossils* (1972), *British Caenozoic Fossils* (1971), British Museum (Natural History). Excellent line drawings of most species occurring in Britain.

Dinosaurs, Swinton, W. E., British Museum (Natural History), 1964.

Evolution of Life, Jarman, C., Hamlyn, 1970.

Evolution of the Vertebrates, Colbert, E. H., Wiley Interscience, 1969. A very readable review of fossil vertebrates.

Face of the Earth, Dury, G. H., Penguin, 1970.

Fossil Amphibians and Reptiles, Swinton, W. E., British Museum (Natural History), 1965.

Geological Time, Kirkaldy, J. F., Oliver & Boyd, 1971.

Handbook of Paleontological Techniques, Kummel, B, & Raup, D., W. H. Freeman & Co., Reading, 1965.

History of the Primates, Le Gros Clark, Sir W. E., British Museum (Natural History).

Invertebrate Fossils, Moore, R. C., Lalicker, C. G. & Fischer, A. G., McGraw Hill, New York, 1952. Contains detailed information on all invertebrate phyla that are represented as fossils. Many good line drawings.

Prehistoric Animals, Cox, C. B., Hamlyn, 1969. A general guide to fossil vertebrates.

Succession of Life Through Geological Time,. Oakley, K. P. & Muir Wood, H. M., British Museum (Natural History), 1964.

The Hamlyn Guide to Minerals, Rocks and Fossils, Hamilton, W. R., Woolley, A. R. & Bishop, A. C., Hamlyn, 1974. Excellent colour plates of minerals and rocks as well as over 250 fossils figured in colour with descriptions.

Treatise on Invertebrate Paleontology, Moore, R. C. (ed.), Geological Society of America and University of Kansas Press, 1953 onwards. Very good books to use for identification as they contain information on all known genera of fossil invertebrates with details of geological and geographical ranges. These books may be consulted at good libraries.

Vertebrate Paleontology (Third Edition), Romer, A. S., University of Chicago Press, 1966. A detailed review of fossil vertebrates giving details of skeletons, teeth and classification.

INDEX

Page numbers in italic
refer to illustrations